A FOX'S TALE

A FOX'S TALE

The secret life of the fox

Robin Page

Hodder & Stoughton

LONDON SYDNEY AUCKLAND TORONTO

British Library Cataloguing in Publication Data

Page, Robin
  A fox's tale.
  1. Foxes
  I. Title
  599.74'442   QL737.C22

ISBN 0 340 38256 2

To my Mother, for her example, her love of animals, both tame and wild, and for the way in which she brought up her own litter.

Contents

Eyes searching the darkness
For light and movement, slow enough for death,
Ears piercing the stillness
For sound and padded silence, the whereabouts of life.
Nose scenting the air
For the hidden patterns of the night.
The fox returns.

He stands alert, surveying time,
Head cocked, enquiring, listening –
Brush combed by a sudden breath of wind;
Beauty and knowledge are combined with speed,
In ruthless harmony.
The fox moves on.

He passes into darkness
As cloud restores the night;
A pheasant calls in warning, of footsteps that bring fear;
The air sighs.
Beneath the trees a shadow hunts,
Time freezes and a rabbit dies;
A dog barks as moonlight falls on blood-stained grass.
The fox has gone.

Introduction

From a very early age foxes have always fascinated me, and this fascination continues as strongly as ever today. My first memory of a fox goes back to when I was under five years old and to the cottage where I was born. It was not an encounter with a wild fox, but the shock of seeing the result of a fox's visit. Several headless hens were heaped up outside the hen-house (a hen-house which is still on the farm today), and without hesitation Father, and Jim, a fine old country-man who worked on the farm, blamed the chaos and carnage on a passing fox. Both told stories of the fox's cunning and I heard more later on, in the classrooms of the village school.

The Hoops, an ancient pub, stood close to the school, and every autumn the forecourt filled with hounds and hunts-men, for a meet of the local foxhunt. Then, much to our amazement, our normally strict head-teacher would tell us to stop work and lead us out of the playground and into School Lane. They were memorable occasions, with red coats in the pub yard, the beech trees turning the colour of old copper, coolness lingering in the air, the smell of horses and the excited hounds anxious to be away. As the hunts-men drank toasts, the whippers-in would crack their whips to control straying hounds, and wagging tails, cold noses, hot breath and long tongues would be all around us.

Those who hunted were a complete mixture: short fat men on long lean horses, men with top-hats, half-moon glasses, one with a monocle, and toothy women with refined voices, who looked as if they might suddenly neigh like their mounts. With a sharp "tally-ho" on the horn and a crack of the whip, the entourage would move off, the horses' hooves clattering on the metalled surface of the road, and several old countrymen with caps, long coats and weatherbeaten faces following behind on their upright bicycles. All day long the occasional sound of baying hounds and the strains of the hunting horn would drift in on the wind, making us wonder what was happening and hope that the fox had got away. One afternoon it was quite clear that the hunt had been outwitted, for so many foxes were put up in an overgrown meadow that the pack and the huntsmen were completely split, with small groups of lost and confused riders and hounds wandering through the village until well into dusk.

Each time I saw the hounds I felt a keen sense of anticipation – would I see a fox? And would it get away? They are feelings that still persist, and whenever I see a hunt in progress I feel compelled to stop, to scan the hedgerows and spinneys for a fleeting glimpse of a russet coat, pointed ears and a white-tipped brush. Part of the fox's appeal is its grace and beauty; but it also has a free spirit, which like that of Man frequently carries it along the fine line between contentment and complete disaster.

It was not until my early teens that I saw my first wild fox, and the occasion remains as vivid in memory as if it occurred yesterday. Since then I have had many encounters and each year they seem to become more numerous. Several fox cubs have lived and shared their lives and secrets on the farm; all gave much pleasure, as well as knowledge, but inevitably the stories of some ended in sadness. One magnificent dog fox returned to the wild, however, and it is highly likely that his great grandchildren still visit the farm at regular intervals and can be heard calling on cold, moonlit January nights.

Some experts have written learned fox books after studying the behaviour of foxes in tennis courts and on leads; in my view they have given much valuable information, but only about foxes in tennis courts and on leads, with the spirit of the truly wild red fox remaining elusive. Because the fox is nocturnal, individual and free, we will never know all its secrets. Consequently recording the life of the fox is like trying to complete a jigsaw puzzle with several of the pieces missing. In the past, country people completed the puzzle with a mixture of folklore and fantasy, much of which is still part of country life today.

This book is not meant to be a definitive study; its aim is to reflect the great joy and pleasure that foxes, both tame and wild, have given me. In several of my earlier books foxes have been a welcome intrusion; here I have allowed them all to meet in one volume, together with numerous others from fact and fiction. I have not tried to find all the missing pieces of the jigsaw, for even now there is still a place for mystery.

Outside, as I write, it is a dark windy night; a distant pheasant calls in alarm and a silent shadow slowly crosses my lawn. For Man it is a time of darkness, but beneath the stars it could be the moment when myth and reality become one.

I

The Fox in Fiction

The first view most people have of the fox is not of the wild fox, but of the "childhood fox", which appears in story-books and nursery rhymes. Consequently its appearance, and the impressions it creates are important, for in later life they can dictate an interest in wildlife, an affection for the fox, and views on hunting. It can also activate the "cuddly bunny syndrome", a condition heightened when Brer Rabbit appears, which gives animals, birds and bees the same thoughts and feelings as human beings.

Most children find the childhood fox a delightful animal, although he is unashamedly wicked, basing his whole philosophy of life on cunning, greed and deceit, yet at the same time he grins, he has a highly developed sense of humour, and those who meet him cannot fail to love him. Indeed, when he is pitted against people, usually farmers and huntsmen, they seem far worse by comparison, and when I was a child I always hoped that the fox would get his way, and he usually did. But although in later years the memories of the childhood fox can distort the view of the real wild fox, it is still a fascinating character in its own right, and some of its activities go beyond fiction, into fable and even into fact.

The first two foxes that I met were both disreputable, but I never tired of hearing about them, at home and at school. They were crafty and deserved their success. One appeared in the old story of *The Gingerbread Man*, when two children went to stay with a little old man and a little old woman on a farm, and as a special treat the little old woman baked them a gingerbread man for their tea. Unlike most gingerbread men, he did not think tea-time was a particularly pleasant part of the day, and so he hopped off the table, ran out of the

An illustration by Randolph Caldecott from The Three Jovial Huntsmen *(Routledge, 1880), showing the way in which the fox traditionally gets the better of the huntsmen.*

open door and away. The little old woman pursued him, the little old man pursued him and the two children pursued him, but he was much too fast and clever for them. Sadly, the world is not a kind place if you happen to be a ginger-bread man, for everybody he met greeted him with the same unwelcome request – "Stop little Gingerbread man and let me have you for my tea." As a result the procession of those in pursuit grew to include not only the little old woman, the little old man and the two children, but also a horse, a cow, a dog and a cat. Tragedy almost struck when the gingerbread man reached a river; there was no boat and he could not swim, for presumably gingerbread men simply become soggy and disintegrate. Luckily a friendly fox came along and offered him a lift saying: "Jump on my tail and I will take you to the other side." Unfortunately as the fox started to swim the gingerbread man began to get wet and so the fox told him to move, first to his back, then to his head and finally to the end of his pointed nose. Suddenly, in a flash, the gingerbread man had gone, the fox had eaten him for his tea. It was a good story; the fox had been thoroughly dishonest and wicked, but the gingerbread man should have known better, and in any case the story had a strange link with country lore. One of the stories told by Father and Jim about wild foxes involved a similar stratagem; if a fox became infested with fleas it would go into a brook or pond leaving only its nose above the surface. When all the fleas were assembled on their small island, the fox would drown them and return to the bank free of all itches and irritations.

The other favourite story involved a small chicken, Chicken Licken, who, after being hit on the head by an acorn, came to the unscientific conclusion that the sky was falling in. As a result he decided that he ought to pass this piece of vital information on to the King. Whenever he met anybody, they asked: "Chicken Licken, where are you going in such a hurry?" And he replied: "The sky is falling down and I'm on my way to tell the King." Another procession started from the farmyard, and it included not only Chicken Licken, but also Henny Penny, Cocky Locky, Ducky Lucky, Drakey Lakey, Goosey Loosey and Turkey Lurkey. Fortunately they met Foxy Loxy who claimed to know the exact whereabouts of the missing monarch: "Follow me," he said, and they followed straight to his den, where his wife and cubs were waiting: "Then the foxes ate Chicken Licken, Henny Penny, Cocky Locky, Ducky Lucky, Drakey Lakey, Goosey Loosey and Turkey Lurkey for their dinners.

"So Chicken Licken never found the King to tell him that he thought the sky was falling down."

At the time, it seemed to me a reasonable way for the fox to get his meal, and in any case it served the assorted farmyard birds right for being so stupid. Again, from observing our own chicken runs it was not at all far-fetched, for over the years we had hundreds of hens, and the kindest thing that can be said about them is that they were not very bright. There was just one exception, Henrietta; for some reason, even as a chicken, she spurned the company of her own kind, refusing to be shut in the hen-house at night, spending her days scrapping around the back door and feeding in the barn on spilt corn and meal. On hot days she would make a dust bath in the drive and if the door of the house was left open she would walk in and stroll about the living room and kitchen, hoping to find crumbs. When the rest of the hens were shut up to lay, she remained free, perching at night in the barn where foxes could not reach her, and long after the others of her batch had gone, she still walked enquiringly into the house, her head cocked slightly to one side as if asking for permission to enter, and her life lasted its full and natural span, which was well over ten years.

One other old story, *The Sly Fox and the Little Red Hen*, contained both an intelligent hen and a piece of country lore. The Sly Fox caught the Little Red Hen by making her dizzy; he ran in circles below her until she fell from her perch, another ruse that is said to be used by wild foxes. All similarity with the wild then ceased, for the Sly Fox put the Little Red Hen in a bag to carry her home. When he stopped to have a sleep, she escaped and filled the bag with stones. On arriving home the Sly Fox boiled some water in readiness to cook his chicken dinner, but instead of the Little Red Hen, stones crashed in, splashing him with scalding water; Sly Fox ran off, out of the district, leaving the little hen to live in peace. I never did like that tale; I felt sorry for the fox and the Little Red Hen seemed much too intelligent for a hen.

The only really disagreeable fox came from another favourite story-book; Beatrix Potter's *The Adventures of Peter Rabbit*. All the rabbits including Peter Rabbit, had to keep a continuous watch for the local fox, a particularly crafty, untidy and unscrupulous creature. He was called Mr. Tod, and foxes are still given the name Tod by country people today, particularly in Scotland and the north.

Other fictional foxes were far more gentle and attractive, such as "The Three Little Foxes" created by A. A. Milne in *When We Were Very Young*:

Once upon a time there were three little foxes
Who didn't wear stockings, and they didn't wear sockses,
But they all had handkerchiefs to blow their noses,
And they kept their handkerchiefs in cardboard boxes.

They lived in the forest in three little houses,
And they didn't wear coats, and they didn't wear trousies.
They ran through the woods on their little bare tootsies,
And they played "Touch last" with a family of mouses.

They didn't go shopping in the High Street shopses,
But caught what they wanted in the woods and copses.
They all went fishing, and they caught three wormses,
They went out hunting, and they caught three wopses.

They went to a Fair, and they all won prizes –
Three plum-puddingses and three mince-pieses.
They rode on elephants and swang on swingses,
And hit three coco-nuts at coco-nut shieses.

That's all that I know of the three little foxes
Who kept their handkerchiefs in cardboard boxes.
They lived in the forest in three little houses,
But they didn't wear coats and they didn't wear trousies.
And they didn't wear stockings and they didn't wear
sockses.

It is interesting to see that in nearly all the illustrations of the childhood fox – "The Three Little Foxes", "Mr. Tod", "Foxy Loxy" and "The Sly Fox" – the fox has a fine white tip to its tail. Our schoolteacher had an explanation for that, too, and it could even have happened in our part of the country, for then every farm in the parish still had its own herd of cows: "Farmer Brown and his wife were milking the cows one morning, when a crafty fox crept up and began stealing milk from the milk churn. The farmer's wife heard lapping and saw the fox drinking, so she chased him from the cowshed. As she went she picked up a bucket of milk and threw it at Reynard; some of the cream landed on the end of his tail, and ever since then the fox has had a white tip to its brush."

In Wales there is a slight variation involving a good Welsh farmer, Farmer Pugh, and the fox, which was not known as Reynard, but by one of its other common names, "Charlie":

One night Charlie was prowling around Farmer Pugh's chicken pen; he was hungry and his hunger was making him careless. As he snooped about the barn he knocked a box of tools off a bench; there was a great clatter, waking up Farmer Pugh, who seized his double-barrel shotgun and rushed outside, wearing his dressing-gown and wellington boots.

The fox ran into the grain shed. Farmer Pugh saw him and followed, waving his gun and shouting. Charlie decided to leave, and as he went he tipped over a barrel of flour, getting covered from the end of his pointed nose to the tip of his tail. When he got back to his den he shook himself, but however hard he shook he could not get the flour from his tail. He even backed into a stream, but the tip of his tail simply floated, and so it has remained white to this day.

It was while in the "Little Room" at the village school that I discovered that foxes had also been involved with other people's tails and had been instrumental in creating the short tail of the bear:

One very cold day a fox saw some fishermen taking home a load of fish. Quietly he jumped up onto the wagon and threw some of the best fish off the back for his dinner.

He was enjoying his stolen meal when an old bear trundled up, and like all bears at that time he had a fine, big, bushy tail: "How did you get those fish?" he asked, "I'd like some for my supper." The fox promised to show him that night, but added: "You don't need a hook and line, I always use my tail." That night they met on a frozen lake and made a small hole in the ice: "Now sit down here," the fox ordered, "and put your tail through the ice – when you feel a lot of fish on your tail, pull."

The poor bear became cold, but whenever he asked if it was time to pull his tail out, the fox told him to stay where he was. Soon his tail was frozen solid, but still he remained sitting. Dogs started to bark and the bear tried to run away, but he was stuck fast. He heaved and heaved, until his tail suddenly broke. The fox rolled over and over in the snow laughing at his trick; the bear was not so pleased, and bears have had short tails ever since.

Once I had risen to the dizzy heights of the "Big Room", I discovered that Brer Fox had used exactly the same trick on Brer Rabbit, changing the rabbit's big bushy tail, to the attractive powder-puff tail of today. My small blue book of Brer Rabbit stories, given to me by a great-aunt when I was seven, remains a much treasured possession. Again the stories showed Brer Fox to be crafty and without scruples, yet each time Brer Rabbit outwitted him, our laughter was mixed with slight feelings of sorrow for Brer Fox.

I had two favourite stories; the best involved the Tar Baby – made by Brer Fox to look exactly like a person. When the Tar Baby failed to respond to Brer Rabbit's "Good Morning", Brer Rabbit hit him, for his lack of manners, and became stuck fast. The more he struggled, the more stuck he became. Brer Fox then appeared to claim his prize, but before eating Brer Rabbit, Brer Fox decided to make him

The wonderful story of Brer Fox outwitting Brer Rabbit by using a Tar Baby.

Brer Rabbit with the upper hand. Brer Fox had intended to unseat Brer Rabbit and eat him, but the spurs proved the stumbling block.

suffer. "But whatever you do," pleaded Brer Rabbit, "don't fling me into the briar patch." Needless to say, Brer Fox threw him into the briar patch, and as soon as he heard Brer Rabbit singing: "Bred and born in a briar patch," Brer Fox knew that he had been tricked. I could see the trick before Brer Fox, for many of the wild rabbits in the parish lived among the briars and brambles of the hedgerows.

In the other tale, Brer Fox decided to allow Brer Rabbit to ride him, like a horse. His plan was to trot off, stop, and then eat Brer Rabbit. Once more the fox was out-foxed, for Brer Rabbit put spurs on his boots, and whenever Brer Fox tried to stop, he received severe kicks in the ribs.

Despite riding Brer Fox, Brer Rabbit did not become a fox hunter, but the influence of hunting crept into the lessons at the village school, for not only did we watch the huntsmen when they met at the Hoops, but we sang with gusto the old nursery rhyme about hunting:

> Oh, a hunting we will go,
> A hunting we will go,
> We'll catch a fox
> And put him in a box
> And never let him go.

We also enjoyed singing the traditional song about John Peel, the famous huntsman from the Lake District:

D'ye ken John Peel with his coat so grey?
D'ye ken John Peel at the break of day?
D'ye ken John Peel when he's far far away
With his hounds and his horn in the morning?
'Twas the sound of his horn called me from my bed.
And the cry of his hounds has me oft-times led,
For Peel's view-halloo would awaken the dead,
Or a fox from his lair in the morning.

At that time too, before vast arable acres had replaced the many meadows and fields of the parish, we could roam freely to play "Fox and Hounds". The "fox" would have a five-minute start and then the "hounds" would set out to search and pursue.

Another popular song was of a fox waking up without the aid of John Peel. It was "The Fox's Foray", printed in full

The hounds do not always get the best of things. This endpaper design by Harry B. Neilson from Sir Francis Burnard's The Fox's Frolic *(1917) sums up the reversal of events.*

towards the end of this book, for all those who want a nostalgic return to childhood. It began:

> A fox jumped up one winter's night,
> And begged the moon to give him light,
> For he'd many miles to trot that night
> Before he reached the Town O!
> Town O! Town O!
> For he'd many miles to trot that night
> Before he reached the Town O!

Children today continue to get much enjoyment from the childhood fox, but as well as the old tales, they have new stories that continue to portray the fox as a crafty, cunning, but easy-going, happy animal. In many, the fox is still trying to outwit man and he usually succeeds, often by plundering his farmyard. Like earlier generations, the modern, more urban child continues to side with the story-book fox.

One of the finest characters is the "Fantastic Mr. Fox", created by Roald Dahl, and in years to come he will be as traditional as Brer Fox and Foxy Loxy. From the beginning there is no doubt about how and where Mr. Fox obtains his dinner:

> "Well, my darling," said Mr. Fox. "What shall it be tonight?" "I think we'll have duck tonight", said Mrs. Fox. "Bring us two fat ducks, if you please, one for you and me, and one for the children." "Ducks it shall be!" said Mr. Fox. "Bunce's best."
>
> But he wouldn't have been quite so confident if he'd known that his three adversaries, farmers Boggis, Bunce and Bean, were lying in wait outside his hole that very night, each one crouching behind a tree with his gun loaded, and each one really determined to shoot him, starve him, or dig him out, even if it took them for ever . . .

His adversaries were terrible men:

Photographs of the fox can often reinforce the crafty, cunning image of the story-books.

Boggis was a chicken farmer. He kept thousands of chickens. He was enormously fat. This was because he ate three boiled chickens smothered with dumplings every day for breakfast, lunch and supper.

Bunce was a duck-and-goose farmer. He kept thousands of ducks and geese. He was a kind of pot-bellied dwarf. He was so short his chin would have been under water in the shallow end of any swimming-pool in the world. His food was doughnuts and goose livers. He mashed the livers into a disgusting paste and then stuffed the paste into the doughnuts. This diet gave him tummy-ache and a beastly temper.

Bean was a turkey-and-apple farmer. He kept thousands of turkeys in an orchard full of apple trees. He never ate any food at all. Instead, he drank gallons of strong cider which he made from the apples in his orchard. He was as thin as a pencil and the cleverest of them all.

Once more, our sympathies are with the fox, not with the hens and ducks he steals, and he certainly lives up to his description – the "Fantastic Mr. Fox".

But the fox in fiction extends further than childhood and there are numerous stories and poems to suit all ages. They cover every aspect of the fox, from its beauty and cunning, to its place in hunting and the traditional English countryside. Old classics concerning the antics and opinions of "Jorrocks" can be read alongside more recent books such as *The Belstone Fox*. In addition there is John Masefield's observant, breathless poem, "Reynard the Fox, or the Ghost Heath Run", as well as the "Fox's Prophecy" of 1871, a poem remarkable, not for its quality, or use of language, but for its feeling and the accuracy of its predictions. It concerns the revelations of an old fox to a huntsman separated from his hounds:

> Then round he turned his horse's head,
> And shook his bridle free,
> When he was aware of an aged fox
> That sat beneath a tree.

It was written by D. W. Nash in Cheltenham and is of interest because of its age and vision. This too is reproduced in full later on.

The reputation of the fox for slyness is not limited to fiction however, and is mentioned several times in the Bible, both in the Old and New Testaments. This shows that the fox's character is not something that has been blackened simply to suit storytellers, huntsmen and poultry farmers, but it has been built up over at least 3,500 years. In the New Testament Jesus calls Herod a fox (Luke 13:32), referring to his cunning and deceit; it is one of the several references which show that Jesus had a great understanding and love of nature and the countryside.

The most interesting biblical record of foxes is to be found in the Old Testament, Judges Chapter 15, verses 4 and 5:

4. And Samson went and caught three hundred foxes, and took firebrands, and turned tail to tail, and put a firebrand in the midst between two tails.
5. And when he had set the brands on fire, he let them go into the standing corn of the Philistines, and burnt up both the shocks, and also the standing corn, with the vineyards and olives.

It is fortunate for Samson that the League against Cruel Sports had not been formed at that time. It is also good to note that the translators used the word "shocks", a local word for me, instead of "stooks" which is used in many other parts of Britain, for standing sheaves of corn.

The Red Fox in Palestine, as known to the early Hebrews.

There are foxes in Israel, but to catch 300 seems a remarkable feat, especially as foxes are usually solitary animals. Alexander Cruden in his *Complete Concordance to the Old and New Testaments* of 1737 explains it quite simply:

> M. Morizon, who has travelled in this country (Palestine), says, that foxes swarm there, and that there are very great numbers of them in the hedges and ruins of buildings. Besides, Samson being so eminent a person, and the judge of Israel, might have employed an abundance of people to catch this great number of foxes, and they might have provided them some time before for his purpose.

Cruden could be right, but in the paragraph before, he probably gets closer to the truth without realising it by saying that in Palestine "there is a kind of creature between a wolf and a fox, which so abounds there, that sometimes troops of two or three hundred of them are to be seen." These were not wolf-fox crosses, but jackals, and it is likely that those involved in the early translations from Greek and Hebrew became confused with foxes and jackals, which still both exist in the area today. They were puzzled too by another Hebrew word translated in the Authorised Version as "dragon"; in later versions, after more knowledge, travel and research, it appears as jackal. It seems therefore, that Samson would have had far less trouble catching 300 jackals. Despite this, tying them together by their tails, whether they were jackals or foxes, to create mobile torches was rather drastic, even if the ploy did create havoc among the Philistines. The Fantastic Mr. Fox would have come up with a better solution.

2

The Fox in Fable

In addition to the Bible, foxes feature in many other old books and stories, where the animal to emerge most clearly and frequently is the fox of fable. Again it is the fox's cunning and roguery that is portrayed, but usually each tale carries a message or warning that can be applied to everyday life. Some of the most famous stories in literary and historical circles are those which make up *The Epic of Reynard*, which were written in France, about AD 1200. They satirised the high and mighty, both people and institutions, with Reynard the Fox representing the church; William Caxton

Below: Woodcut from a chapbook edition of Reynard the Fox *(1780). Only the fox's tail distinguishes it from the simplified cat.*

Above left: An elaborate woodcut illustration from an edition of Aesop published in Naples in 1485, showing the story of "An Ape and a Fox".

printed his English translation in 1481.

Geoffrey Chaucer also used a fox in "The Nun's Priest's Tale", one of his *Canterbury Tales*, and again Sir Russel Fox was used to warn readers of dangers that could befall them at any time. The main message was to be on guard against those who flatter in order to deceive, and it was the fox who was doing the deceiving. He had been attracted to a yard by the crowing of a cock "Chanticleer", when the boasting bird suddenly noticed the approach of danger:

And so it happened as he cast his eye
Towards the cabbage at a butterfly
It fell upon the fox there, lying low.
Gone was all inclination then to crow.
"Cok cok," he cried, giving a sudden start,
As one who feels a terror at his heart,
For natural instinct teaches beasts to flee
The moment they perceive an enemy,
Though they had never met with it before.
This Chanticleer was shaken to the core
And would have fled. The fox was quick to say
However, "Sir! Whither so fast away?
Are you afraid of me, that am your friend?"

The fox then proceeded to praise the voice of the cockerel's father, before asking: "Can you not emulate your sire and sing?" The request, aimed at the bird's vanity, had exactly the desired effect:

This Chanticleer began to beat a wing
As one incapable of smelling treason,
So wholly had this flattery ravished reason.
Alas, my lords: there's many a sycophant
And flatterer that fill your courts with cant
And give more pleasure with their zeal forsooth
Than he who speaks in soberness and truth.
Read what Ecclesiasticus records
Of flatterers. 'Ware treachery, my lords!

This Chanticleer stood high upon his toes,
He stretched his neck, his eyes began to close,
His beak to open; with his eyes shut tight
He then began to sing with all his might.
Sir Russel Fox then leapt to the attack,
Grabbing his gorge he flung him o'er his back
And off he bore him to the woods, the brute
And for the moment there was no pursuit.

Eventually, men and dogs sorted themselves out and gave angry chase, and despite the uncomfortable nature of his enforced ride, Chanticleer, hearing help on its way, managed to outwit Sir Russel Fox, but only just:

Chaucer's Chanticleer also appeared in the Reynard Story. This drawing by Frank Calderon comes from the edition of Reynard the Fox *edited by Joseph Jacobs (Macmillan, 1895).*

This cock that lay upon the fox's back
In all his dread contrived to give a quack
And said, "Sir Fox, if I were you, as God's
My Witness, I would round upon these clods
And shout, 'Turn back, you saucy bumkins all!
A very pestilence upon you fall!
Now that I have in safety reached the wood
Do what you like, the cock is mine for good;
I'll eat him there in spite of every one.'"
The fox replying, "Faith, it shall be done!"
Opened his mouth and spoke. The nimble bird,
Breaking away upon the uttered word,
Flew high into the tree-tops on the spot.

So the fortunate cockerel, with more brain power than
Chicken Licken, escaped. The fox tried to trick him down,
once more, but Chanticleer had learnt his lesson. Not only
was the bird unusual in managing to escape from the jaws of
a fox, but due to Chaucer's desperate search for a word to
rhyme with "back", he became the first and last cockerel
ever heard to "quack".

The most famous and best loved fables are those of
Aesop, probably a Greek peasant, which date back to AD 500
or even earlier. I heard them too in the village school and
particularly enjoyed those involving foxes. Inevitably each
fable showed the fox's cunning; sometimes used for good,
but usually intended to deceive.

The story that caused me the most amusement was one
involving a fox and a stork. The fox wanted to be seen as a
good neighbour, but he was also very greedy. Consequently,
shortly after the stork's arrival for the summer, the fox
invited her into his earth for supper. On the table was a large
flat dish of delicious broth from which the fox lapped
eagerly; with her long pointed beak the stork was unable to
get one drop. The next day the bird returned the compli-
ment and invited the fox round to her nest for a meal and he
accepted, still amused at his own cleverness. When he
arrived the stork produced a beautiful meal, served in a

A fox cub – they are usually born in litters of four or five.

Caught in mid-yawn!

pitcher with a long thin neck. The stork ate her fill, slowly and politely, using her slender bill skilfully, while the fox looked on with his mouth watering; sadly, his nose was too wide for the pitcher and he was unable to reach even the smallest crumb.

The fox's appetite features again, when he manages to outsmart a crow in much the same way that Chanticleer out-thought Sir Russel Fox. This time the fox saw a crow sitting up a tree holding a piece of tasty looking cheese in its beak. The fox thought for a moment and then said: "What a magnificent bird you are, Mr. Crow. If only you could sing we would want you to be our king." The crow was flattered and wished to show immediately that he did have a fine voice to match his appearance; he began to caw, but as soon as he opened his beak the cheese fell to the ground and the fox had an easy snack. The fable shows that beauty without brains is not much use.

"The Fox and the Stork" from the 1485 Italian edition of Aesop.

On another occasion the fox's appetite gets him into serious trouble, but at the same time teaches a very useful lesson. He was feeling hungry when he found that a shepherd had left his dinner hidden in a hollow oak. The fox crept in and ate the bread and cold beef at his leisure, before having an after-dinner nap; although he had eaten at mid-day the fox still called the meal "dinner", as it was his largest feed of the day. He had not yet been influenced by the modern affectation that turns every mid-day meal into "lunch". On waking he tried to get out of the hole, but much to his alarm he had eaten so well that he was stuck. Another passing fox heard the commotion and looked in; seeing the greedy fox's predicament he said: "Don't worry, stay there until you are as thin as you were when you went in, then you will be able to get out quite easily." The moral of this fable is simple – time helps to solve difficult problems. Although the message is meant for human ears it seems that foxes have also heard it, for when hunting or trying to rob a farmer's hen-house, many foxes show that they are prepared to be extremely patient, as well as cunning.

Another fable could also apply to wild foxes, and is probably the most famous story of them all – the fable of the "Fox and the Grapes". Again a fox was out hunting when he saw a bunch of sweet, ripe grapes hanging down from a vine

The famous fable of "The Fox and the Grapes" as illustrated by Thomas Bewick, the great eighteenth-century naturalist and wood engraver.

close to the path. He loved grapes and so stood up on his hind legs to try and reach them, but they were too high. Even when he jumped they remained just out of reach, although on one occasion, with his greatest effort, he managed to touch the lowest grape, with his wet nose, removing the bloom. He finally gave up, saying to himself as he walked away: "It doesn't matter, they were not ripe and I don't like sour grapes anyway." The story has an important message, that people often blame circumstances, instead of their own inefficiency or lack of ability. It also shows that Aesop was well acquainted with the habits of foxes, for in warm climates they enjoy grapes. This is confirmed in the Bible too, where in one of the most beautiful love poems ever written, "The Song of Solomon", it says: "Take us the foxes, the little foxes, that spoil the vines; for our vines have tender grapes," (Chapter 2, v. 15) – implying, it seems, that foxes can cause problems in vineyards when the grapes are ripe.

Like many storytellers, Aesop frequently used the fox's cunning to make his point. By the time the poor old fox had struggled out of the hole in the oak tree he was very thirsty, and in his eagerness to drink he fell into a tank of water. Unfortunately the sides were too high for him to get out and he was well and truly stuck. Soon a thirsty Billy-goat came along and asked the fox if the water was good. Reynard immediately seized his opportunity: "It's wonderful; so clear, cool and refreshing, why don't you get right in like me." Without hesitation the goat jumped in, but as soon as his thirst had been satisfied, he realised that he could not get out. The fox had a good idea; "Why don't you stand near the edge of the tank, then I will climb on your back, get out, and then pull you out." This they agreed to do and the fox was soon on the bank and making for home. "What about me?" bleated the goat. The fox was not impressed: "You have more beard than brains," he said scornfully, "You should have thought about how to get out, before you jumped in." It is a wise story, for sensible people seldom begin anything, unless they can see all the options. Some foxes heed the

"The Fox and the Goat" as portrayed by the Flemish engraver, Marcus Gheeraerts the Elder, from an edition of Aesop published in Bruges in 1567.

same fable, for it is very unusual for a fox to get into a poultry house, without being able to get out.

The voice of experience is repeated in a tale involving a lion, a donkey and a fox, who agreed to go hunting together. At the end of a successful day the lion told the donkey to share out the spoils and the donkey duly obliged, dividing the game into three equal parts. The lion was not pleased and instead of thanking the donkey, he jumped on it and killed it. He then told the fox to share out the food. The fox was a fast learner and quickly made a large heap for the lion and a small one for himself. "Why did you do that?" the lion asked. "Look what happened to the donkey," the fox replied. It is a story showing that we can learn from misfortune. There is no doubt that foxes learn quickly; hence the old proverb: "A fox is not taken twice in the same snare."

In one story, Aesop seems to owe something to the Old Testament and Samson, but with very different results. A farmer became so angry at the disappearance of his hens that he set a trap for the guilty fox and caught it. Not satisfied with this he wanted revenge, so he tied straw to the fox's brush and set fire to it, before releasing the poor animal. The fox ran off in alarm, right through the farmer's fields of ripe wheat – the fields blazed and the farmer lost his entire harvest. It is another good message: that revenge can be a two-edged sword. Fortunately the fox shows little sign of ever taking revenge, something that cannot be said for those from whom he steals hens, ducks, turkeys and even ornamental wildfowl.

In addition to Aesop's Fables there are numerous other fox stories, by a variety of writers, but unfortunately they are very difficult to classify accurately or fairly. Many were written as "fact" but read like "fiction"; consequently the only kind description for them is "fable". They were written by the early naturalists, and most contain passages of accurate observation; however, nearly all of them include much more, for the philosophy of the early writers seems to have been: "When in doubt make it up." As a result their natural histories are every bit as entertaining as Aesop's Fables and

A delightful woodcut from an encyclopaedia by "one of the early naturalists", Edward Topsell's History of Four Footed Beasts *of 1558.*

contain foxes that could even teach the Fantastic Mr. Fox new tricks. They reveal some normal patterns of fox behaviour, but then fact and folklore drift into the realms of sheer fantasy.

One of the worst offenders was Oliver Goldsmith, for not only did he write poetry about the rural scene, such as "The Deserted Village", but he also wrote what he considered to be serious books on natural history, including *A History of the Earth and Animal Kingdom*. Sadly for his reputation, he was a much better poet than naturalist, as he shows when writing about the fox, for he decided there was not just one type of wild fox in Britain, but three – "only three":

> There are only three varieties of this animal in Great Britain, and these are rather established upon a difference of size than colour or form. The greyhound fox is the largest, tallest and boldest; and will attack a full grown sheep. The mastiff fox is less, but more strongly built. The cur fox is the least and most common; he lurks about hedges and out houses, and is the most pernicious of the three to the peasant and the farmer.

News, or plagiarism, travelled fast in those days for Goldsmith's three foxes appeared in 1855. They re-appeared in 1860 in a book by John Sherer entitled "Rural Life"; he too claimed that there were three types of fox: "The Greyhound Fox", "The Common Fox", and the "Little Red Fox". Oliver Goldsmith would not have been too upset, for it is widely accepted that he also "borrowed" much material from other writers.

Goldsmith's general description of the fox is interesting and quite accurate, but by the end, he has allowed fancy to take over:

> The Fox is of a slenderer make than the wolf, and not near so large; for the former is above three feet and a half long so the other is not above two feet three inches. The tail of the fox is longer in proportion, and more bushy; its

The fox (bottom right) interestingly placed within the dog family in Mrs. Pilkington's edition of Oliver Goldsmith's Animated Nature *(1807).*

nose is smaller, and approaching more nearly to that of the greyhound, and its hair softer. On the other hand, it differs from the dog in having its eyes obliquely situated, like those of the wolf; its ears are directed also in the same manner as those of the wolf, and its head is equally large in proportion to its size. It differs still more from the dog in its strong offensive smell, which is peculiar to the species, and often the cause of their death. However, some are ignorantly of the opinion that it will keep off infectious diseases, and they preserve this animal near their habitations for that very purpose.

The fox has since the beginning been famous for his cunning and his arts, and he partly merits his reputation. Without attempting to oppose either the dogs or the shepherds, without attacking the flock or alarming the village, he finds an easier way to subsist, and gains by his address what is denied to his strength or courage. Patient and prudent, he waits the opportunity for depredation, and varies his conduct with every occasion. His whole study is his preservation; although nearly as indefatigable, and actually more swift than the wolf, he does not entirely trust to either, but makes himself an asylum, to which he retires in case of necessity; where he shelters himself from danger and brings up his young . . .

He generally keeps his kennel at the edge of the wood, and yet within an easy journey of some neighbouring cottage. From thence he listens to the crowing of the cock, and the cackling of the domestic fowls. He scents them at a distance; he seizes his opportunity, conceals his approaches, creeps slyly along, makes the attack, and seldom returns without his booty. If he be able to get into the yard, he begins by levelling all the poultry without remorse; and carrying off a part of the spoil, hides it at some convenient distance and again returns to the charge . . .

In the same manner he finds out bird's nests, seizes the partridge and the quail while sitting, and destroys a large quantity of game. The wolf is most hurtful to the peasant, but the fox to the gentleman. In short, nothing that can be eaten seems to come amiss; rats, mice, serpents, toads and lizards. He will, when urged by hunger, eat vegetables and insects; and those that live near the sea-coasts will, for want of other food, eat crabs, shrimps, and shell-fish. The hedge-hog in vain rolls itself up into a ball to oppose him: this determined glutton teases it until it is obliged to appear uncovered, and then he devours it. The wasp and the wild-bee are attacked with equal success. Although at first they fly upon their invader, and actually oblige him to retire, this is but for a few minutes, until he has rolled himself upon the ground and thus crushed such as stick to his skin; he then returns to the charge, and at last by perseverance, obliges them to abandon their combs; which he greedily devours, both wax and honey.

In much the same way Alexander Cruden allows fancy to replace fact in his *Complete Concordance*, making it rather too "complete":

Many things are said concerning the craft and subtilty of foxes. They lay their dung in the entrance of the badger's den, and by that means obtain it for their own use. They fright the wolves, who are their enemies, from their dens, by laying the herb sea onion at the mouth of them. They dig holes for themselves, but then they leave several outlets, that if the huntsmen lays his snare at one, they may escape at the other. When sick, they eat the gum of pine trees, whereby they are not only cured, but their days lengthened. It is said, that when they are pursued by hunters, they make urine on their tails, and strike them upon the dog's faces. Some having been taken in a gin by the leg, have bit it off, and so escaped; others have feigned themselves dead, till they have been taken out, and then have run away. Being hungry they feign themselves dead, on whom the fowls lighting for prey, they snatch and devour them. Many other things are storied of their cunning.

A Fox's Tale

Even more respected country writers get lured into the same trap including Charles St. John, a well known nineteenth-century sportsman and naturalist. In his *Natural History and Sport in Moray* he reports:

> If a fox finds a rabbit at a sufficient distance from the cover, he catches it by fair running; but most of his prey he obtains by dint of numberless stratagems which have earned for him a famous, or rather an infamous, reputation from time im-memorial. From what I have myself seen of the cunning of the fox, I can believe almost any story of his power of deceiving and inveigling animals into his clutches. Nor does his countenance belie him; for handsome animal as he certainly is, his face is the very type and personification of cunning.
>
> The cottagers who live near the woods are constantly complaining of the foxes, who steal their fowls frequently in broad daylight; carrying them off before the faces of the women, but never committing themselves in this way when the men are at home. From the quantity of debris of fowls, ducks etc, which are strewed here and there near the abodes of these animals, the mischief they do in this way must be very great.

The foxes who visit our hen-houses are far less discerning for they will steal hens or guinea fowl regardless of the sex of those working on the farm or in the farmhouse garden. In his *A Tour in Sutherlandshire*, Charles St. John claims that he does not normally record fictional accounts of the fox, but then, in the next sentence relates a story that I find difficult to believe:

> The foxes in the Highland districts must frequently be put to many shifts for their living, and no doubt become proportionally cunning. To keep himself in the fine and sleek condition in which a fox always is, many a trick and ruse de guerre of surpassing cleverness must be practised. The stories of their manoeuvres to catch animals

are endless; and, though many of them would be amusing enough, I do not like quoting as facts incidents of this kind, the authenticity of which I cannot vouch for, however much I may believe them to be true, and I must confess to being very credulous on this point. I have been assured by a person not given at all to exaggerate nor easily deceived, that he once witnessed the following trick. Very early one morning he saw a fox eyeing most wistfully a number of wild ducks feeding in the rushy end of a Highland lake. After due consideration, the fox, going windward of the ducks, put afloat in the loch several bunches of dead rushes or grass, which floated down amongst the ducks without causing the least alarm. After watching the effects of his preliminary fleet for a short time, the fox, taking a good-sized mouthful of grass in his jaws, launched himself into the water as quietly as possible, having nothing but the tips of his ears and nose above water. In this way he drifted down amongst the ducks, and made booty of a fine mallard. Though this story seems extraordinary, it must be remembered that the fox manages to capture wild ducks, woodpigeons, hares and numberless other animals, sufficient to keep himself and family; and it is self-evident that in doing so he must practise many a trick and manoeuvre that would seem most improbable if related, and quite beyond the instinct of animals. I have seen one in confinement lay out part of his food just within reach of his chain, in order to attract the tame ducks and chickens about the yard, and then, having concealed himself in his kennel, wait in an attitude ready to spring out till some duck or fowl came to his bait, which he immediately pounced upon. Those, too, who have trapped foxes can tell of the extreme cunning and sagacity displayed by them in avoiding danger. In fact, altogether a fox in a state of nature is as interesting an animal as he is beautiful, and nothing can exceed the grace and ability of his movements when he is hunting, or playing unobserved, as he fancies, by his enemy man. It has happened to me frequently to have opportunities of watching a fox, and I have always been unwilling to put a stop to my amusement by shooting him, which, in a country where hounds cannot be kept, one feels bound to do, as a punishment for the endless mischief which he commits.

It is easy to mock these earlier writers, but we do so unfairly, for in general our present-day understanding of foxes is only based on the accumulated knowledge and findings of others, and it is still incomplete. It is a pity though, that people like Oliver Goldsmith and Charles St. John should litter their facts with folklore, making their natural histories quite unnatural. It does mean, however, that their work is far more readable and entertaining than some of the dry and serious tomes produced today in the name of "science", "ecology" and "environmental studies"; perhaps Aesop, Brer Rabbit and Cruden's *Concordance* should become essential reading at all University departments of animal behaviour.

Reynard gets the goose again. A Thomas Bewick woodcut.

3

The Fox in Folklore

Like the foxes of fiction and fable, I met the fox of folklore at
a very early age, and I still regularly meet him today, for he is
alive and well and living where he has always lived, in the
minds and recollections of country people. It is pleasing that
he continues to flourish, and he can be encountered at any
time, in ordinary conversations, proverbs, superstitions and
traditional beliefs that are said to explain some of his more
remarkable exploits and achievements.

The first story I heard again came from Father and old
Jim on the farm, to show how a fox managed to catch hens or
pheasants perching high in a tree. It was the same method
used by the Sly Fox to catch the Little Red Hen, and
apparently modern-day foxes still use it. Once the bird is
located the fox runs round and round in circles until the
unfortunate hen gets dizzy, and falls to the ground.
Although the bird gets dizzy, it is never explained how the
fox prevents itself from getting dizzy.

The other method used by the fox to get a perching fowl
was to walk underneath the branch slowly, so that the
watching bird gradually overbalanced. There is no doubt
that roosting hens do get taken by foxes and we have lost
many on the farm, as well as guinea fowl, that were last seen
high up in fruit trees, and elms. Then, after dark, a commotion has indicated something strange happening and in the
morning the birds have disappeared. Some people simplify
the disappearance of perching poultry by asserting that
foxes can climb trees, almost as well as cats.

Equally common are the stories explaining how foxes rid
themselves of fleas, and it does seem to be a fact that foxes
seldom have fleas or lice. They kill rabbits and hedgehogs,

which are usually "lousy", but somehow the fox remains flealess and I have never seen a flea on either a dead or live fox. Gamekeepers, naturalists, huntsmen and fox owners all confirm their usually flealess state, most telling variations of the same story; they believe it too, and I was first told the tale as "fact" by an old countryman: "When a fox gets over-populated by fleas, it will go and gather some sheep's wool

"The Fox and the Crow" by Edward Griset from a Victorian edition of Aesop's Fables.

and carry it to a river in its mouth. It will then slowly walk into the water, until only the wool is showing. When all the fleas have gained refuge on the wool, the fox will let it float away." A doctor from Kent heard the story from a friend of his in Ireland, who actually claimed to have seen the fox perform the trick. But the doctor was not totally convinced: "One has to take into consideration that my friend was well known for his high intake of poteen."

In other variations the fox uses a piece of wood instead of wool, or simply lets the fleas settle on its nose before submerging completely.

Foxes are also supposed to use water to unroll hedgehogs, for they appear regularly on the fox's diet. On finding a curled up hedgehog Reynard is said to roll it to the nearest pond or stream and into the water. As soon as the hedgehog uncurls in order to swim, leaving its underside without protection, the fox makes its attack.

The method for catching hares is simpler and drier. Jim believed that foxes caught hares when "ol' Sally" was sitting in her form, simply by approaching from the front. According to him there were two reasons for this; firstly hares spend much time in their forms looking behind them, so they can often be approached directly. And secondly a hare always runs forwards from its form; consequently if the fox gets close enough, the hare runs towards it initially and its chances of escape are reduced as a result.

Archibald Thorburn the artist, records something totally different in his book of mammals, first published in 1920, with the fox making a form, but unfortunately his source was not too reliable:

Various are the ruses employed by the fox when hunting his prey. Charles St. John in *Natural History and Sport in the Highlands*, describes how at day break he once watched one planning an attack on some hares feeding in the open, first preparing an ambush by scraping a hollow in the ground where he knew by instinct his quarry would pass when leaving the field after sunrise. As soon as a hare came sufficiently near his post, Reynard by a sudden rush seized and killed her immediately.

Thorburn also mentions a sighting of his own:

At times the Fox employs entirely different tactics, and will apparently make use of the curiosity or liability to fascination in the nature of any bird or other animal he may wish to circumvent. As an instance of this, while walking some years ago along a Hampshire lane in June, my attention was attracted by the unusual crowing of a cock Pheasant among some tall grass in a meadow on the other side of the hedge. On making my way through a gap I saw a Fox some thirty yards away from the bird, circling around his prey yet without appearing to notice it. The pheasant, although quite aware of his enemy's presence, was making no attempt to escape, and I think the fox was trying to approach near enough for a sudden spring, when they both saw me and each made off.

This coincides closely with a common story in which the fox chases his tail until he attracts an audience of rabbits, hens or geese. When they get within striking distance he gets an easy dinner. It is a form of the old warning proverb: "When the fox preaches, take care of the geese."

Another proverb linked to the fox's hunting habits is very widely believed: "Foxes prey furthest from their earths."

To confirm this, countrymen will quote numerous examples of rabbits and foxes living happily side by side, and also of pheasants hatching and rearing large broods close to a fox's earth. Consequently a hungry fox is said to move quickly into his neighbour's parish to hunt: "A fox never speeds better than when he is on his own errand."

By so doing he creates havoc away from his own territory, and gets other foxes the blame. If the plundering fox is then followed back to its den by an irate farmer, hen owner, or gamekeeper, he should heed another old warning: "Woe to the fox that only has one earth."

The fox in farmland, blending in with the landscape.

A lazy indolent pose, the type that reinforces the fox's storybook reputation for cunning.

The dog-like characteristics of the fox can be clearly seen here and such examples fuel the controversy about dog-fox crosses.

Those who have been robbed and seek instant revenge are advised to slow down and let their anger cool, for: "A fox fares best when he is most curst."

Instead they should take note of three wise sayings: "With foxes we must play the fox," "A fox knows much, but more he that catcheth him," and "He that would deceive a fox must rise betides."

In bygone days, once a fox had been caught its brush was often hung up above the door of a stable or cow shed to help keep off evil and bring good luck. This probably originated from the old belief that witches could turn themselves into foxes although most witches preferred to appear as hares. Those who set out to snare foxes should be very careful when approaching their victims, as there is a very peculiar old belief that: "If bitten by a fox you will die within seven years." An elderly farm worker disproved this story locally, when he set a snare in the bottom of a ditch, close to a spinney, in what he thought was a hare run. Checking it the next morning, he saw animal movement and, assuming that he had been successful, he fell on the snare intending to kill his victim. Much to his surprise it was a fox that slashed his hands with panic-stricken bites. Seven years later he was still telling the story. His fox did prove another belief, so it is claimed, for foxes sometimes pretend to be dead when caught. The old man, not wanting to lose his prey tried to throttle it until all resistance stopped. He took the body out of the snare and laid it down while he studied his damaged hands. Having patched them up with his handkerchief, and feeling pleased with his efforts, he bent down to pick up the corpse by its brush, but it had gone, having quietly recovered and slunk off into the trees.

John Clare, the nineteenth-century Northamptonshire poet, obviously believed that foxes were capable of this deception, for he described it in one of his poems:

The shepherd on his journey heard when nigh
His dog among the bushes barking high
The ploughman ran and gave a hearty shout

A Fox's Tale

He found a weary fox and beat him out
The ploughman laughed and would have ploughed him in
But the old shepherd took him for the skin
He lay upon the furrow stretched and dead
The old dog lay and licked the wounds that bled
The ploughman beat him till his ribs would crack
And then the shepherd slung him at his back
And when he rested to his dog's surprise
The old fox started from his dead disguise
And while the dog lay panting in the sedge
He up and snapt and bolted through the hedge . . .

When faced with other circumstances, the fox will adapt its cunning accordingly. It is said that a poisoned fox will look for the herb hyssop; while if it tastes the poison and manages to vomit immediately, it will never be fooled by a poisoned

Tales of foxes feigning death are common and here is a twelfth-century illustration which proves the point.

bait again. Some huntsmen claim that a hunted fox will seek out and shelter under a juniper tree, for the strong smell obliterates its scent and also confuses the hounds.

But of all foxes, it is the old fox that is said to be the wisest and the most cunning, hence: "Old foxes want no tutors," "A fox might change his skin, but not his manners" – and "An old fox is hardly caught in a snare."

Because of the fox's reputation, John Gay wrote a poem "The Fox at the Point of Death", about an old fox that almost changed its ways; almost, but not quite.

> A fox in life's extream decay,
> Weak, sick and faint, expiring lay;
> All appetite had left his maw,
> And age disarmed his mumbling jaw.
> His num'rous race around him stand
> To learn their dying sire's command;
> He raised his head with whining moan
> And thus was heard the feeble tone.
> Ah sons, from evil ways depart,
> My crimes lye heavy on my heart.
> See, see, the murdered geese appear!
> Why are those bleeding turkeys there?
> Why all around this cackling train,
> Who haunt my ears for chicken slain?
> The hungry foxes round them stared,
> And for the promised feast prepared.
> Where, Sir, is all this dainty cheer?
> Nor turkey, goose, nor hen is here:
> These are the phantoms of your brain,
> And your sons lick their lips in vain.
> O gluttons, says the drooping sire;
> Restrain inordinate desire;
> Your liqu'rish taste you shall deplore,
> When peace of conscience is no more.
> Does not the hound betray our pace,
> And gins and guns destroy our race?
> Thieves dread the searching eye of power,

And never feel the quiet hour.
Old-age, (which few of us shall know)
Now puts a period to my woe.
Would you true happiness attain,
Let honesty your passions rein;
So live in credit and esteem,
And, the good name you lost, redeem.
The counsel's good, a fox replies,
Could we perform what you advise.
Think, what our ancestors have done;
A line of thieves from son to son;
To us descends the long disgrace,
And infamy hath marked our race.
Though we, like harmless sheep, should feed,
Honest in thought, in word, in deed,
Whatever hen-roost is decreased,
We shall be thought to share the feast.
The change shall never be believed,
A lost good-name is ne'er retrieved.
Nay then, replys the feeble Fox,
(But hark! I hear a hen that clocks)
Go, but be mod'rate in your food;
A chicken too might do me good.

There are in addition pieces of peculiar folklore, quite
unrelated to the fox's age or bad habits. One requires an
intimate knowledge of both foxes and the weather before it
can be proved or disproved, for: "When spots of rain fall and
the sun is shining, a fox is getting married." Unfortunately I
have never seen foxes during a sunshiny shower, but their
study would make a good subject for a large thesis and an
equally large research grant. In addition foxes can be used in
straightforward long-range winter weather forecasting, for:
"If foxes bark much in October they are calling up a great
fall of snow." They also appear in country medicine, as a
cure for whooping cough. If a fox visits the farmyard or
garden regularly, a saucer of milk should be left out for it; in
the morning the patient must drink whatever is left. If foxes

are not available, then ferrets make a good substitute, and the smell is even worse. If the fox actually comes into the house, then the treatment can stop – it is a sign of imminent death. In Wales, it is a good sign to see a single fox, but unlucky to see several together.

The origins of these beliefs are difficult to see, but it is easy to explain one other old saying, borrowed by Oliver Goldsmith: "The wolf is most hurtful to the peasant, but the fox to the gentleman." When wolves roamed wild they were a great danger and could threaten the peasant's livelihood by stealing his livestock, whereas the fox mainly threatened the gentleman's "sport" by taking his pheasants. There is an old, bad poem, that suggests pheasants were also hurtful to the peasant:

Old Farmer Hubbard
Went to the cupboard,
To get his poor dog a crust
When he got there
The cupboard was bare.
"Drat them pheasants," he cried, "they've been fust."

Mary, Mary, quite contrary,
How does your garden grow?
"Well the mangolds are pecked,
And the whole place is wrecked,
It's those damnable pheasants you know."

Jack Sprat could get no fat,
His wife was just as lean,
For those wretched peasants
Were worried by pheasants,
From morn till dewy e'en.

Some of the most pleasant old beliefs link foxes with wild flowers. One of my favourite flowers, purple loosestrife, is also known as "foxtails" because of the shape of its flower-heads. The grass, meadow foxtail and the false fox sedge are both common in ditches and wet meadows, and when

flowering and seeding they too resemble a fox's tail. In the West Country red valerian is a well known, attractive plant and the Somerset name for it is "fox's brush". Other parts of the fox's anatomy are also remembered, hence the early purple orchid is known as "fox stones", because its tubers are said to resemble the testicles of a fox. In Lincolnshire toadflax is called "fox and hounds" and in some areas the beautiful white but thorny burnet rose is known as the "fox-rose". Possibly this name comes from the fact that the rose grows where foxes are common, on downs, heaths and dunes. In Northern Europe bluebells are also known as "foxbells". At one time foxes were hunted enthusiastically for their tails, to ward off evil. Because of this they asked God to help them and he obliged by putting the "bells" on bluebells. Now, whenever hunters pass by, the flowers ring out in warning.

Orange-hawkweed is often known as "fox and cubs", but the most famous fox plant is the common foxglove, which among its numerous country names includes "fox-and-leaves", "fox-docken", "fox-fingers", "foxy", "fox's glove" and "foxter". Another name is "fox-flops", suggesting that it grows from fox droppings; this means there must be thousands of foxes in some areas.

Foxgloves are commonly found thriving in the disturbed soil around a fox's earth and so the association between flower and fox is very close. The name foxglove is thought to have a simple origin, for foxes were said to wear a flower on each paw, to help them go about their business more silently. I can imagine "The Three Little Foxes" of A. A. Milne's poem wearing foxgloves, but I have never seen a fox wearing them, and those that visit our hen-houses seem to get on very well without them.

Legends about foxes and their habits have lent themselves to associations with wild flowers. From top left to right: Purple loosestrife – "foxtails". Early purple orchid – "fox stones". Toadflax – "fox and hounds". Red valerian – "foxbrush". Burnet rose – "fox rose". Foxgloves.

4

The Fox in Fact

It seems incredible to me now, that I did not see my first wild fox until I was in my early teens. An occasional one would visit the farm at night, under cover of darkness, and there were obviously enough to satisfy the hunt, but in general they were few and far between, bordering on scarce. Times have changed, for every year, for several years, I have had numerous encounters with foxes and their numbers still seem to be increasing.

The reason for their earlier scarcity is easy to explain. Then, many people in the parish kept hens, not on a commercial scale, but just a handful of free-range fowl in runs at the bottom of their gardens, to provide eggs for their families. Consequently foxes were unwelcome guests and any intrusion would lead to snares and traps being set. This was not confined simply to my village, it was common practice all over the country in rural areas. In addition, rabbits were so plentiful that rabbit-trappers regularly worked the warrens and hedgerows, and again foxes were not welcomed. If a trapper arrived early one morning to find that a fox had removed a rabbit before him, traps would then be set for the fox, and this was at a time when fox furs were fashionable with many women. As a result foxes were under great pressure and, ironically, for most of the year they were far safer living on the farms and estates of keen foxhunters, where they were given a degree of protection. In places, foxes became so scarce that foxhunters actually imported large quantities from France to replenish numbers.

Change came in three phases during the 1950s and each one reduced the pressure on the fox. Social and financial changes meant that fewer people bothered, or needed to keep hens – it was easier, and sometimes cheaper, to buy eggs from shops. This removed the danger of the back garden snare.

Then in 1953 myxomatosis arrived in Britain, sweeping from one end of the country to the other within two years, and rabbits disappeared from the countryside. It was so devastating on our farm that we actually thought the rabbit had become extinct, a fact that greatly saddened us. At first glance such a catastrophe for the rabbit was also bad news for the fox, as it removed an important item from the fox's menu. But more importantly it made rabbit-trapping a complete waste of time and so more assorted snares and traps were removed from the hedgerows, and the major threats to the fox had vanished. At about the same time gin traps, which took a heavy toll of foxes, were made illegal, removing yet another danger. So, possibly for the first time in centuries, the fields, hedgerows and country gardens became reasonably safe places for foxes to live or visit. As a result the population rapidly expanded, and areas that once seldom saw foxes gradually filled up with them. The population spread so fast and so far that the wild red fox of the English countryside even became urbanised and spread into many of our towns, both large and small.

Scientists claim, quite rightly, that the fox's success is based on its "adaptability". They mean that its diet is wide and varied, and not just rabbits, but often they overlook the changes that allowed the fox to live in safety and "adapt".

The sighting of my first fox came shortly after myxomatosis had cleared the rabbits from our land. I was out for a Sunday afternoon walk with the dogs, through the "brook meadows" – old grass meadows that follow the meanderings of the narrow brook, which forms the southern boundary of the farm. Suddenly, there on the far bank, in an arch of hawthorn and bramble, was a fox; we stood still – both surprised – staring at one another. It was even more beautiful than I had imagined; its coat the same colour as autumn leaves in sunlight, complete with a fine white tip to its tail. It was autumn, but overcast, yet to my eyes its welcome

A typical scavenging urban fox.

presence seemed to glow. Soon it had seen enough, turned and disappeared from view. The meeting left me elated and its memory continues to give me pleasure. After that, sightings were infrequent, but gradually they became more regular, until now they are a common occurrence. Familiarity has not bred contempt, however, for I still experience a thrill of excitement and anticipation whenever a fox appears and each year I learn something new concerning their private lives.

There have been many ordinary but memorable encounters; one was again in the brook meadows, in early summer, with the field awash with growing grass. It was a fine fox, a deep-russet red, once more with a white tip to its brush, and it was hunting. When it reached some bushes it started to look up into the branches as if searching for birds' nests, sometimes standing up on its hind legs to get a better view. With the wind carrying my scent away, I was able to walk slowly, to within a few feet of it.

My closest view occurred during a beautiful sunlit October dawn, when I had gone to an ancient wood to watch the rut of the fallow deer. I was walking along a small woodland path when I heard a woodpecker busily hammering bark, high up in some old ash trees, and I followed the sound to see the bird at work. Standing by a small clump of hazel I could see nothing in the boughs above, just dappled patches of bronze and copper from the rising sun. Below, and forty yards away, the copper light caught and coloured the movement of a rich chestnut coat; I was downwind from a fox and it was weaving its way through brambles and dewberries straight towards me. It was in perfect condition, sleek, fit and unhurried. Only four yards away it stopped and squatted down – it was a vixen. Her brown eyes were clear and deep and she gazed up in relief, straight into my face. She looked, thought, and suddenly her brain processed my presence, for a look of panic flooded her expression and she fled, with her ears turned back.

I have been as close to cubs, again in the early morning, when I was checking an earth in our largest field. After several minutes of watching and seeing nothing I walked

Three fox cubs.

over to one of the entrances. As I looked in, a small cub, not more than a month old, looked out. The sun was rising behind me and I froze. Slowly the cub emerged, followed by two more. They rolled, fought, yawned and scratched, sometimes running to within a yard of my feet, without the slightest interest in me, until my effort to remain motionless began to hurt. I moved a foot slightly, and all three immediately heard and saw movement and disappeared.

One of my most amusing encounters involved the same earth, when I decided to stand in a hedge bordering the brook meadows about forty yards away from the holes, hoping to see cubs. It was a warm cloudy evening in early May, about an hour and a half to sunset. There were no signs of foxes and all was quiet except for the birds and the drone of distant tractors working until the last of the light. Yellowhammers and larks were singing and suddenly the warning cry of a blackbird rattled out. What caused its alarm I could not see and I wished that I possessed the knowledge of some old gamekeepers who claim to be able to tell what disturbs a blackbird by the tone and the intensity of its alarm signal. The grating calls of partridge carried from beyond the brook and a cock pheasant strolled over close to the earth. It stood erect and called, flapping its wings as it did so, rather like a cockerel crowing; no rival replied and so it walked through the hedge and out of view.

Within yards of the earth's main entrance a rabbit with her three young ones were out feeding. Occasionally they would run and jump in play, their white "cotton-tails" showing up clearly in the fading light. Rabbits and foxes live side by side in this hedge most springs and it seems to confirm that foxes really do "prey furthest from their earths".

A rustle betrayed a rabbit leaving the hedge a few yards away from me; it was so close I could actually hear it nibbling grass. After biting off several stalks it would sit up with four or five long pieces of grass hanging from its mouth; then without using its front paws, it would chew quickly and the grass would be drawn into its mouth until it disappeared, almost as if it was saying "look no hands". From time to time it would sit up, working its ears in all directions for danger and looking straight at me, yet it was not alarmed, showing that stillness can be a most effective and simple form of camouflage. Eventually it moved off and I decided to measure the distance it had been from me – a mere eight paces. Eight yards out into the field I looked up, and there, sitting, looking at me through the long grass, was a full-grown fox. Its ears were upright and its eyes were full of enquiry. We studied each other briefly, before it quietly turned and vanished into the hedge without any sign of panic. I had seen no cubs; I had been seen, and I felt satisfied with an evening well spent. Perhaps the cry of the blackbird had warned of the fox observing me, well before I had seen it. If so I was watched for a long time. Like some present-day game-keepers, Oliver Goldsmith believed that birds have a special warning cry for "fox":

> For the birds who know him for their mortal enemy, attend him in his excursions, and give each other warning of their approaching danger. The daw, the magpie, and the blackbird, conduct him along, perching on the hedges as he creeps below, and with their cries and notes of hostility, apprize all other animals to beware, a caution which they perfectly understand and put into practice.

A friend, who is a warden of a famous bird reserve, once witnessed a far less alert blackbird. In the middle of the afternoon he saw a fox wandering over a field erratically, repeatedly changing direction and behaving as if it was performing a strange eccentric ritual. As it progressed over the field a number of birds mobbed it, including a foolish blackbird; as its unusual movements continued, so their caution disappeared, until the fox suddenly reverted to normal – it turned and sprang, and in a flash, the blackbird had become a mid-afternoon snack.

The fox's year is an interesting one to follow. It begins in January with the mating season, and I often stand outside on clear, frosty evenings, listening for a tell-tale bark, for it is the breeding season when barking foxes are most commonly heard. "Bark" is not really a good description, for it sounds nothing like the bark of a dog; it is shorter, more guttural and mournful; indeed on a cold moonlit night it has an extremely eerie quality. Between 1406 and 1413 Edward III's grandson, Edward, second Duke of York, wrote *The Master of Game*. In it he describes the fox's bark, but whether he is correct to ascribe it to the vixen I do not know. "And when the vixen is assaute, and goeth in her love to seek the dog fox she crieth with a hoarse voice as a mad hound doth, and also when she calleth her whelps when she misses any of them, she calleth in the same way."

The vixen is on heat for about three weeks, but pregnancy can only be achieved during a brief three-day period. Many country people argue about foxes; some say the animal they most resemble is the cat, while others insist that they are more like dogs and even claim the existence of fox-dog crosses. The way in which foxes mate could well provide the answer, for one side or the other, but unfortunately few people have seen a pair of wild foxes locked in passion, and I certainly have not.

Six years ago a local farmer was lucky; it was a cold damp morning in January when he noticed a fox walking alongside a hedge close to his farm. It disappeared briefly, but quickly re-emerged and began to walk towards the middle of the field. Suddenly another fox came from the hedge and followed about fifteen yards behind. The tails of both animals were twitching from side to side, almost like a slow-motion wag. Once in the middle, the vixen stopped and the dog approached and mounted her. Over the years the farmer had lost a lot of poultry and he ran for his rifle. When he returned the pair were "knotted", back to back like dogs, and from a range of two hundred and fifty yards he let fly. "You should have seen them. They didn't know whether they were coming or going. It took them about ten seconds to separate, a bit quicker than dogs, and they were gone."

Since then my brother John has seen the same thing. It was day-break and he was cultivating during frost, when through the mirk he saw a strange animal in the centre of the field. It looked as if it had a head at each end and a tail in the middle. Three-quarters of an hour later as the light improved he could see that the "animal" was in fact two foxes, locked together back to back. He stopped the tractor and walked towards them; he approached to within thirty yards when they managed to force themselves apart and run off.

Some "experts", and non-experts, claim to be able to tell the difference between dog foxes and vixens in the field, but it is a skill I have never been able to acquire. Various measurements of head and body are sometimes given, usually in centimetres and kilograms, standards that I do not understand anyway. It seems a pity that one of Britain's "traditional" animals has to be described in untraditional metric measurements, instead of feet and inches, pounds and ounces. For those, like me, who have no intention of making the change, a dog fox is normally heavier than a vixen, with the average weight being about 14 lb, although some go well over 20 lb. The average vixen weighs about 12 lb. Foxes are most often seen singly and so in any case I cannot tell whether they are large or small, male or female, for there is usually no other animal present for comparison.

To hear people talk, there are far more dog foxes than vixens, for each story about a fox begins: "I saw a large dog fox the other day." During a hunt, one upper-class Master of Hounds was irritated by his village roadman, for when the hounds had run out of scent, the old man, who had been watching the proceedings while leaning on his broom, suddenly shouted: "A dog fox over there. A dog fox over there!" And he pointed away from the hounds. The Master evidently considered that a non-hunting roadman was incapable of sexing foxes and he asked with disdain: "How do you know it's a dog fox?" "Because when it jumped the gate, I heard its balls rattle," came the instant reply.

Fortunately foxes can tell the difference between male and female without the aid of centimetres or five-bar gates,

A romanticised Victorian view of a vixen and her cubs, which appeared in the Illustrated London News *in May 1893.*

and the resulting cubs are usually born in March after a gestation period of about 53 days. There will normally be four or five cubs to the litter, although families reaching double figures are not unknown. Their eyes open after ten to fourteen days and they begin to venture above ground towards the end of April or early May. That is the best time to go "cub-watching", when the surrounding vegetation is quite low, so allowing good views. It is also the best time to see the items on the fox family's menu, for the area around the earth will be littered with remnants – rabbits, rats, hens, or whatever is available or preferred. Hares and pheasants are usually to be seen too, confirming that foxes do commonly catch hares, although the hare has an obvious advantage in speed. But how does the fox catch the hare, and is there truth in the old beliefs? Some people think that the increase in fox numbers has led to the dramatic reduction in the size of Britain's hare population over recent years. It seems to me, however, that the hare's demise must be attributed not simply to the efficiency of the fox, but also to the over-use of agricultural sprays, and to the changing fashions of farming.

The pheasants caught include both cocks and hens, yet the cock bird does not help to incubate the eggs (on the ground) and so, are they made to topple over while roosting at night? I frequently hear the alarm calls of pheasants after dark, during all seasons of the year but have no idea how the cocks get taken; whether by stealth, deception, or cunning. Whenever old Jim saw a tail-less pheasant, he always claimed that it was a fortunate bird that had just managed to escape the jaws of a fox. Some foxes have been seen to steal pheasants the easy way. They have suddenly approached during a shoot and made off with a shot bird, before it could be picked up by a dog or a "beater".

Occasionally the remnants of a hedgehog may be found close to the entrance of an earth, showing that foxes do manage to take them. For a brief period of two summers, I found the remains of many dead hedgehogs along the brook meadows. It seemed to me that a fox had acquired both the taste, and the knack of opening them. Although the meadows run alongside the brook, there was never any indication of the hedgehogs being rolled into the water. Since then I have seen few victims, as if the fox concerned has died, moved on, or developed a taste for other things.

I watch fox cubs most years and strangely, although many

reliable fox-watchers have seen both dogs and vixens bring-
ing food to the young, I have never seen more than one adult
at an earth with cubs; a situation observed by others too.
Because of this it seems to me that there is no hard and fast
rule; sometimes the vixen is left to bring up her family by
herself, while others receive help from their mate, or even
from a vixen without cubs.

The largest family I have watched consisted of six cubs, in
a pleasant east-facing earth, on a grassy bank. The cubs
were half-grown, and despite the large size of the litter they
were fit and well fed. From a distance of thirty yards I
watched them fight, stalk, pounce, jump and roll together in
vigorous play. Suddenly they stopped, looked and bounded
off down a gentle hill towards the middle of the field. From
the greetings, whimpers and whines, similar to the noises
made by my pet foxes, I assumed it was the vixen returning
with food. Carefully and slowly I moved, to get a better view,
but the old fox must have seen me, for she screamed in
warning, sending the cubs scampering back to the earth and
underground.

The scream of a fox, much shriller than its bark, is quite
blood chilling to those who do not recognise it. On a
beautiful mid-summer evening I was walking through the
fallow deer wood with my brother and his wife, when a fox
screamed within a few yards of the woodland ride. The
scuttling of feet through the undergrowth indicated a vixen
and her cubs; to my sister-in-law it was something unknown
– violence or murder – she nearly died of fright.

All during the summer it is possible to get unexpected
views of cubs; stalking beetles by the roadside; romping on
haybales, or chasing butterflies. As the season moves on and
the crops, grasses and hedgerow flowers get higher, so
sightings become fewer. The youngsters grow quickly, and
often they lie out all day in the corn, until it is time to resume
hunting at dusk. During most harvests our combine puts
several cubs and adults out of the rapidly diminishing areas
of standing wheat and so they return to their holes and
hedgerows. As soon as the straw is baled, fox droppings

appear on the heaps of bales, showing clearly the fox's inquisitive nature and also its favourite late summer food; for the "scats" contain blackberry pips, the indigestible wings of black ground beetles, damson stones, and sometimes whole sloes, as well as traces of fur and small bones.

As I write this chapter, we are busy carting bales of straw in the aftermath of harvest and there seems to be a surplus of food available this year. On one heap of bales I found a dead shrew, killed but uneaten, as if foxes dislike the taste, in the same way as cats. Numerous mice have also been left, some being battered and damp, like playthings. Most have had their heads removed; it is another peculiarity of the fox that one of its hallmarks is to leave its victims headless, whether hens, pheasants or in this case, mice. The dark coloured droppings again reveal that blackberries, beetles and damsons are more popular than mice at the moment. It seems that the harvest mouse-hunting is mainly a source of amusement, as it is with the farm dogs – digging and searching in the stubble for hours on end.

During autumn and early winter, some foxes still prefer to stay in the open fields, basking in the weakening rays of the sun while lying in stubble or in a comfortable ploughed furrow. For several years, we had an old grey fox that would lie out on the ploughed land of our largest field. During the day it would casually watch the tractor working its way up and down, and at night it was often seen around the village, scavenging from gardens and dustbins. Although grey with age the fox always looked to be in good condition, until one autumn it failed to appear in its usual place, and we did not see it again. It was a large fox, and its relaxed manner and fine coat seemed to verify that: "An old fox need not be taught tricks."

Its habit of raiding dustbins as soon as they were put out also confirmed the proverb: "Like a fox, grey before he is good."

Old grey foxes are not uncommon and Charles St. John saw both old foxes and elderly eagles, although how he could identify an ancient eagle I have no idea. He wrote:

A pet dog fox aged thirteen years.

The foxes' faces being gray and their jaws nearly tooth-less; yet they were still in good, and even fat condition. In animals, age and cunning supply the place of strength and activity; so that the eagle and fox are still able to live well, even when they have arrived at the most advanced age assigned to them.

The fact of the old fox going into the village to scavenge, is not a surprise. For some time I pedalled around the parish early in the morning as part-time postman, before returning home to write and work on the farm. I often saw foxes in all parts of the village and one morning there was even one sitting outside the post office itself. That is why the town fox does so well, for dustbins, gardens, urban parks and rubbish tips can provide a plentiful supply of food.

Our neighbouring farmer, who saw the mating fox, has also had foxes lying out in the fields watching him work in the autumn. One even developed the habit of following the plough – eating the disturbed beetles and mice as it went.

In winter the fox is never far away. Several times I have disturbed animals that have been sleeping in trees, so proving the story that foxes can climb. Although farmers may lose their poultry to foxes at any time, it is in December that losses can be particularly damaging, when turkeys and cockerels are being fattened for Christmas.

Again our neighbour had a strange experience. Shortly before Christmas a fox broke into his turkey shed, killing fifteen fat turkeys. It took one to eat and left fourteen bodies, dead and uneaten. The next day the tractor driver was cultivating in a nearby field when he drove right over a resting fox, rolling it over several times with his spring-tined harrows. Apparently undamaged, the fox slowly stumbled off; it was not sick or injured, but bloated.

5

The Fox and the Fowl

It is the fact that foxes raid hen-houses and chicken-runs throughout the year that makes them so unpopular. They are unwelcome to shepherds, too, at lambing time, as well as to gamekeepers and nature reserve wardens, when ground nesting birds are trying to incubate their eggs and rear their young. Sadly, foxes are not conservationists – to them, terns and avocets are as acceptable as pheasants and hens. Again, if foxes simply took the odd bird or lamb, they could be tolerated, but unfortunately they indulge in what is known as "surplus killing". If they get into a hen-house they can leave virtually all the occupants dead; while if they visit a tern colony, they will simply "chop" the sitting birds at random.

The "experts" have various theories about "surplus killing". Some say that in a hen-house the fox panics when confronted by all the squawking and flapping, leaving death and destruction behind as a result. Others say that the killing is done on purpose, with the fox intending to return for its victims, to bury them for later use. In my view there is an element of truth in both claims, but the main reason is far more simple. Several years ago I saw "surplus killing" actually taking place. We had experienced a spate of raids by foxes, early in the morning; it was a well worn procedure; the hens crying out in alarm, the dogs barking, and me stumbling out of bed to make sure no damage was being done.

Again, just after dawn, a tremendous commotion broke out at the deep-litter shed. I looked out of my bedroom window; the door of the shed had burst open, hens were everywhere and a fox was rushing around in the nearby horse-radish, among the feathers and fowl, having a wonderful

70

time. From the movement of the large leaves there could have been several foxes – possibly a vixen and cubs. I rushed down and soon all was quiet, with sixteen bodies and many feathers showing where the entertainment had been. Far from showing signs of panic, the fox I had seen was clearly enjoying itself – it was playing. With movement and feathers it had been chasing and pouncing. Many dogs play all their lives; fox cubs play and my pet adult foxes loved to play. Consequently I am certain that play is a major factor in the "surplus killing" involving foxes. I suppose if it had been given a Latin name and linked to a fashionable jargon word and first mentioned in a PhD thesis, then scientists would have accepted it long ago. So, until surplus killing has officially been labelled "ludat interacti" the "experts" will continue to look for much more complicated and less likely explanations.

The worst case of surplus killing on the farm happened ten years ago. When Father went to feed some pullets on "the point of lay", he found that a hole had been scraped underneath the hen-house door and inside twenty-eight birds were scattered about dead, some headless and some with their necks broken. A few nights later I was disturbed by hens in the deep litter crying out, and two eyes reflected back through the window of the shed when I shone my torch. The fox jumped up and scrambled out through the already barred window, and inside another twenty-nine hens were dead. Most of the fifty-seven birds killed were in good enough condition to pluck and eat, and we gave many of them away to friends, but on a small family farm it meant a significant loss of eggs and income that Father and John could not afford.

An even worse example came from a council house garden in the village High Street. There, the owner of the hens had sixty-two killed in a single night, out of a total of seventy. They were littered all over neighbouring lawns and the street itself. When the owner, who no longer keeps hens, heard that I was writing a book about foxes he said: "I suppose you are saying how lovely and friendly they all are."

Then he added, almost poetically: "In my opinion, the whole . . . lot, should be . . . well shot."

From the fox paths behind the farm, foxes visit the farmyard on most nights. They seem to look over the whole place and we have even found fox droppings on the cattle yard roofs. Once we had free-range hens and loose Muscovy ducks, but as fox numbers increased the hens were shut up and all the ducks were stolen and eaten, despite our efforts to protect them. We had many guinea fowl taken too, and if the fox had a choice between a guinea fowl, hen or duck, it was always the unfortunate guinea fowl that was taken. Now, if a guinea fowl or hen gets out and it is not recaptured before nightfall, it will have disappeared by morning.

Our saddest fox casualty was an old gander who lived on the farm with its two mates for twelve years. He arrived on the farm unannounced and uninvited during the freezing winter of 1962–63. A smallholding was deserted by its owner, and rather than stay behind and starve, as did many hens, the geese walked down the road and into the farm-yard, where they established their new home. He was often at the gate in his favourite puddles or grazing on the grass verge, and most passing motorists would stop to let him cross the road with no signs of irritation. At night the geese were never shut up, and whenever they cackled we assumed that they were seeing off a fox or an uninvited prowler, for they made excellent "watchdogs".

If they saw Cassius, my tame fox, they would open their wings, stretch up to their full height, and make as much noise as possible. The display worked, for Cassius would not go near them.

Gradually time caught up with the old gander; his liking for puddles gave him rheumatics and he gradually lost the sight of one eye. As a result it was possible to walk almost up to him from one side, without being seen. A vixen with cubs evidently did the same thing, and one morning he was missing. He had not gone far; because of his size he had been dragged under a weeping willow tree in the garden and half eaten. The family returned the following night to finish their meal, and thereafter, the wing-feathers were used as playthings and changed position nearly every night. We missed the old gander, but his offspring still puddle about the yard and roadside verges, slowing down the traffic, and they still refuse to be shut in at night.

It is not only farmyard geese that get taken, for wild geese also get caught. Again during the summer of writing this little book, a dog fox near the Minsmere bird reserve, in Suffolk, caught three adult Canada geese and two shelducks, to take to his vixen and cubs. He carried them at least a quarter of a mile, which is no mean feat, as the shelduck is the largest British duck, and a Canada goose can weigh well over eleven pounds. It is interesting to speculate how the geese and ducks were carried. There are countrymen who

The fox in pursuit of geese by the light of the moon from the Illustrated Sporting and Dramatic, *1887.*

claim to have seen ducks carried like the grey goose in the Fox's Foray:

> He took the grey goose by the neck,
> And swung him right across his back.

Exactly what else is stolen from the farm we do not know. The dogs love hen food, and so if foxes go into the barn and feed from a sack, we would never know. Eggs get taken regularly too, indicating that either the foxes get into the hen-houses, or some hens get out; nearly every year we find eggs buried in the farmhouse garden. They are usually in perfect condition, without a mark or a crack; from the smell of fox that is often found with them, they have almost certainly been buried by foxes for later use. To those unfamiliar with it, the smell of a fox is a very difficult to describe. It is strong, lingering, and not totally unpleasant, rather like the smell of urine after asparagus has been eaten.

During some years the local foxes cause great problems, ripping boards out of hen-houses to get at the hens, or trying, sometimes successfully, to climb in through the windows. Once break-ins occur, they usually get worse, as if the fox responsible develops an insatiable appetite for hens. Unfortunately, when that happens, the only solution is to remove the troublesome fox.

At other times, although foxes obviously still visit the farm, we get little or no trouble, suggesting that the foxes in residence prefer other food. At the time of writing we have had few raids in three years, and so we have been able to leave the foxes in peace. This too, is something that the "experts" often ignore – for like dogs, cats, and humans, individual foxes have their own likes and dislikes when it comes to food. Consequently if a gamekeeper complains that foxes live solely on pheasants and other game, both his natural history and his competence are highly suspect. Similarly, if an apologist for the fox suggests that it eats nothing but creatures harmful to the farmer, such as rats, mice and slugs, then he too obviously prefers fantasy to fact.

Some apologists even say that voles are the main food of foxes. If that was so there would be very few foxes, for the vole population is notorious for running in cycles; suddenly there will be a great population explosion, and then numbers will plummet just as fast.

During a vole glut in Windsor Great Park, a gamekeeper, now enjoying retirement watching birds and making homemade wine, caught a fox. It was so fat that he thought it was pregnant at the wrong time of the year. When he carried out a postmortem he discovered that it had gorged itself on 203 young mice and voles. It had found an ideal field of rough grass with many tussocks of cock's foot, full of vole runs and nests. Like me, the old gamekeeper believes that a fox's diet depends on personal taste, the season, and the availability of food. When food is short they will eat carrion; in the autumn they like wild strawberries, blackberries and rowan berries, and at other times they will take mice, moorhens, rats or pheasants, depending on mood and opportunity.

In areas of sheep farming, some foxes develop a liking for lambs, although "unscientific" scientists and assorted "experts" claim that only the weak are taken (all newly born lambs are weak), suggesting that the lambs would have died in any case. This is doubtful, and suggests that the experts do not like accepting the abundant evidence available from unlettered farmers, shepherds and country people. Numerous farmers have seen quite healthy lambs taken, presumably at a time when the "experts" are usually still in bed. One farmer in the Lake District had a problem when a fox developed the habit of killing lambs simply to get at their livers. While a countryman in Lancashire found an earth where the cubs were being fed almost exclusively on lambs, with the remains of twenty-one scattered about near the earth.

To old countrymen the fact of foxes taking lambs was widely accepted, hence: "The fox barks not when he would steal the lamb." Similarly, in the sixteenth century Thomas Tusser had the following advice for farmers during the month of March:

75

Keepe sheepe from dog,
Keepe lambes from hog,
If foxes mowse (bite) them,
Then watch or howse them.

It is odd that some "experts" accept that newly born, healthy deer can be taken by foxes, but they deny the same fate for lambs – yet most lambs at birth are smaller than freshly dropped fawns. Experts also accept that foxes take hares, and again, hares are both faster and heavier than lambs – so why is there a reluctance to admit that foxes take lambs?

There are even extreme cases of foxes killing grown sheep and I know of one pet fox that escaped and killed a full-grown Soay sheep. In his "A Tour in Sutherlandshire", Charles St. John came across cases of full-grown sheep being taken: "It is not the general custom of foxes to destroy the old and full-grown sheep where lambs are plentiful; but a colony or pair of foxes having once commenced this habit, the mischief and havoc which they commit are beyond calculation, more particularly as they seldom tear or eat much of so large an animal, but feed on the blood. According to the accounts of shepherds the foxes of Ben Laighal are very prone to this kind of prey, and kill the old sheep in preference to lambs or game."

But although hens and lambs are sometimes taken, it should be remembered that the fox's diet varies – it has always varied and it will always vary. The variety was known to the Duke of York as long ago as the fifteenth century, when he wrote of the fox:

He liveth on all vermin and all carrion and on foul worms. His best meat that he most loveth are hens, capons, duck and young geese and other wild fowls when he can get them, also butterflies and grasshoppers, milk and butter. They do great harm in warrens of coneys (rabbits) and of hares which they eat, and take them so gynnously (cunningly) and with great malice and not by running. There be some that hunt as a wolf and some that go nowhere but to villages to seek the prey for their feeding. As I have said they are so cunning and subtle that neither men nor hounds can find a remedy to keep themselves from their false turns. Also foxes commonly dwell in great hedges or in coverts or in burrows near some towns or villages for to evermore harm hens and other things as I have said. The foxes' skins be wonderfully warm to make cuffs and furs, but they stink evermore if they are not well tanned.

The diet of the modern-day fox can have one or two strange additions. A fox owner in County Durham had a vixen cub that developed a liking for dirty clothes: "One thing she did in particular was to find a shirt or sweater recently discarded, and suck the armpit area, or suck a pair of socks. She won't suck clean socks or sweaters; this led me to believe that she did it for salt."

An engineer from Kent had an equally interesting experience:

In 1972 I was working on the construction of the M27 motorway, which involved reclaiming about four hundred acres of Portsmouth Harbour. Initially the silt was dredged off the sea bed, and then chalk embankments built out in a defined pattern, and finally the areas between the embankments filled in with chalk to differing levels to form the motorway earthworks. Some of these embankments linked with Hornsea Island where there were foxes, and thus gave them access to our work areas.

We worked on a shift basis, with shift A on for twelve "day" hours and shift B for twelve "night" hours, changing each week. After we had been there for some time, in early summer (either May or June) a fox with three cubs was regularly seen, and soon encouraged by the workmen. The men would leave food near their tea hut, and later the four foxes (particularly the cubs) would approach the hut at tea break, and would accept food thrown to them, coming as close as perhaps twenty feet. However, they would only do this for the men on shift A, and despite similar encouragements from shift B, would have nothing to do with those men at all. On Mondays when the shift pattern changed it took the foxes a while to adjust to the timings of the new week, but then they would settle down to approaching shift A again. This went on for about three months until the pattern of work changed and the tea hut was removed, after which I never saw the foxes again.

During this period, a feature of the work was that we isolated areas of water by our method of placing chalk, and for short periods created lakes of salt water, which contained fish, cut off from the sea. One morning I saw a young fox standing at the edge of such a lake and darting forward to snatch at something so that his whole head went under water. I was in a Land Rover on a track some ten feet above him, which caused him no alarm at all. Though I could not see into the water I can only assume that he was fishing. I watched him for some ten minutes, after which he wandered off on to Hornsea Island and I lost sight of him.

In folklore foxes are said to fish successfully with their tails, and in real life there are numerous reports of foxes scavenging on the sea shore, eating crabs and shellfish, but this is the only case, I have heard of, involving sub-aqua diving tendencies. However, the fact of a fox putting its head under water does not surprise me. We once had a border collie on the farm, called Foss; she loved water and would regularly put her head under to retrieve stones thrown into the shallows of the brook.

It has to be admitted, however, that foxes do not spend all their time having tea-breaks and fishing, and they can cause problems on farms and nature reserves. But despite their unfortunate activities, their other characteristics, and their beauty, still make them a very welcome part of the country scene.

6

The Fox in the "Fog"

Despite the fact that foxes appear to have a character almost entirely their own, there are people who insist that in many ways foxes resemble cats; while others maintain that they are in reality very close to dogs. The theory concerning cats is very hard to follow; the similarity is said to come from the fox's elliptical pupils, its ability to climb trees, and the fact that when it sleeps it wraps its tail around its body, like a cat.

These are not very convincing similarities; a wolf has elliptical pupils, but few people would confuse a wolf with a cat. It is true that foxes climb trees, but their methods are most uncat-like; their claws are not retractable and they rely almost entirely on speed, agility and balance. My present dog, Bramble, a little lurcher, a cross between a whippet and a Bedlington terrier, is also a good climber, but he too relies on agility and balance. The trees most commonly climbed by foxes are old elms, willows and ashes, with grooved bark and plenty of nodules and branches to assist. Quite often the trees are hollow, with the foxes scrambling up the inside of the trunks, before venturing out to lie on a branch. Both hunted foxes, and those simply resting, have been seen in trees, well over twenty feet from the ground. The fact of a fox wrapping its brush around itself during sleep is most unsurprising, for especially in winter it must be extremely cosy and create good insulation.

But although a fox cannot realistically be compared with a cat, the relationship between foxes and cats is an interesting one. Our farm cats must regularly see foxes and when I had a tame fox the cats simply arched their backs and spat at it. Yet some cats do get taken and I have seen the body of a large black cat outside an earth; whether it was a road casualty and scavenged, or hunted and killed, there was no way of telling. Once cats were deliberately put down earths, for an old country method of flushing a fox is to "stick a stinking dead cat down the hole".

On the farm, during a period of fox raids, we experienced a strange incident involving a small, dark, short-eared cat. She kept coming into the house meowing and rubbing herself against our legs as if she was trying to tell us something. It was unusual, for normally she kept entirely to the farmyard, spending most of her days hunting mice and rats, and only going to the old granary at feeding time. With her tail erect and meowing loudly, she led us to an old bale stack and a hole in the bales. I felt inside and my hand rested on something damp and cold. I pulled out the bodies of three kittens, all dead, and again she meowed as if beseeching us to restore life. All the kittens had their necks broken, one was headless and another had a lump eaten out of its rear. The dogs could not have been responsible, for that part of the bale stack was too insecure and it seemed to be the work of a fox. I buried the kittens, but the cat's sorrow did not cease for several days. On several nights she climbed through my bedroom window, jumping on to my bed wanting fuss and reassurance. Gradually her need for human company and consolation left and her territory again became the farmyard.

An animal ecologist from the north of England saw one of his cats actually being chased by a fox one spring morning. When he went outside with his dog the chase stopped immediately and the cat reached safety. Later in the day he heard a commotion and a fox had one of his semi-tame geese by the neck, and as it tried to run it was being pecked and buffeted by the other geese. Again, when his dog started to bark the fox dropped the goose, which apart from bruising and lost feathers was unhurt. Two days later a goose was stolen and so efforts were made to catch the determined fox. It turned out to be a very old, thin vixen with badly worn teeth.

But if foxes chase cats, cats also chase foxes. An old man in the next village claims to have seen a large ginger Tom

A dog in a hollow tree, appearing to be very comfortable, with its brush wrapped around it.

chase a fox out of his garden and along the High Street in broad daylight. Elsewhere, in Shropshire, a tortoiseshell cat and a fox were seen together, apparently hunting voles, while two foxes and a cat were seen together by a car driver near Bury St. Edmunds:

> One night last July about 11 o'clock I was driving down a private farm road and, as I turned the corner, I saw on the road about 200 yards away three pairs of greeny coloured eyes about two or three yards apart. As I got nearer in the headlights I saw that one was an adult fox, one was a half-grown cub, and one was a large black and white cat (I have seen the cat round these meadows before) and he undoubtedly comes from a house about a quarter of a mile away. I presume he is a big old Tom.
>
> On the left of the road was a field of uncut wheat having 4′ high sheep wire netting down the side, and on the right was a meadow. As I got nearer, the old fox jumped over the wire netting, and I could see his beautiful brush as he sailed across. The cub and the cat trotted down the road side by side. When the cub turned and saw the old fox missing he too jumped the wire and went into the wheat, and the cat turned at right angles and went across the meadow towards his home.
>
> It appears that these three were merely having a friendly meeting. They were not stalking each other or fighting.

At a Bradford scrapyard, a cat and a fox also met. The fox was wandering around near a warehouse, when it saw one of the warehouse cats. It walked over to it, sniffed it all over and then just trotted away.

None of my pet foxes liked cats, or resembled them in any way. My last vixen however could be very dog-like. When she was pleased she would wag her brush in exactly the same way as a dog and when bored she would chase her tail. If given a rat she would shake it with a movement that in the wild would have meant instant death to a rat or a rabbit. On a lead she would hunt, and on locating mice or voles she would dig rapidly and enthusiastically; she reminded me of an excitable collie or Shetland sheepdog.

But although in many ways she reminded me of a dog, she would not respond to orders: all attempts to house-train her failed, and when out on her lead she pulled almost continuously. She could hear the faintest sound in the grass, but not the word "heel". She got on well with the farm dogs, but at the approach of strangers she would hide under her box. On the occasions when she escaped she failed to respond to calls and only returned after several days, when she felt like it. At that time Foss was the farm border collie and the similarity between the two was remarkable, right down to the white tips to their tails.

If my old vixen was dog-like, Bramble, my lurcher, is almost fox-like. This is particularly apparent when he is trotting over the fields with a precise destination in mind, usually rabbit holes, for his head is held high and his whole manner is exactly like a fox. Similarly, when movement attracts his attention he freezes, with one fore paw held off the ground just like a fox. Mouse hunts in old grass are also fox-like, for he dives with his front paws after sound and movement.

Because of this uncanny likeness, this behaviour raises the question of whether a domestic dog can mate with a wild fox, and what would the offspring be called. When a Dachshund crosses with a Corgi, the resulting mongrel is apparently known as a "Dorgi", so presumably a dog-fox cross would be called a "Dox" or a "Fog". For many years there have been rumours of fox-dog crosses, but so far all the evidence is hearsay, with no little "doxies" or "foggies" actually being produced with one parent yet alone two. Thomas Bewick the great eighteenth-century naturalist and wood engraver claimed to have seen a litter: "We have also seen sharp nosed dogs, called fox-dogs, and were at the same time assured that they were a cross between the two animals; but it has always so happened that the assertion could not be substantiated."

Oliver Goldsmith was quite adamant however: "The fox,

Evidence for the dog-fox cross comes from a Landseer drawing taken from the Annals of Sporting and Fancy Gazette, *July 1824, showing "a cross of the dog and fox in the possession of Lord Cranley".*

though resembling the dog in many respects, is nevertheless very distinct in his nature, refusing to engender with it."

Much more recently, in the seventies, there were reports of fox-dogs at Glen Trool in Galloway, described as black labrador-like animals called "Ramasites"; but again the exact parentage could not be proved, although they were said to have had a wild, foxy appearance.

Because of the similarity between collies and foxes, I am sure that a friendly female collie and an amorous dog fox could mate, but in normal circumstances such a union is highly unlikely. The fox is naturally extremely cautious and many working dogs develop a great antipathy for foxes. Despite all the doubts, another eye-witness account of a fox-dog cross came a few years ago from a neighbouring village, where an old retired poacher-cum-gamekeeper

claimed to have seen a litter. His father was a shepherd and
bought a new sheepdog:

> That was a lovely thing though. It had some puppies an'
> that was the one that got crossed with a blinkin' fox. One
> frosty night in January, very frosty an' moonlight, when
> my father was expectin' some early lambs, his ol' bitch
> was in season. An' he'd see these ol' foxes muckin' about,
> a night or two before, and so he thought: "I'll try those ol'
> foxes," 'cause he was up to everything my father was. An'
> he took this ol' bitch when it was getting dusk and kept
> walking her about where he'd seen these ol' foxes. An'
> that was a real moonlight night an' he staked her out in the
> field, so he could see her from his shepherd's hut. An' he
> sees this ol' fox makin' to her an' it kept goin' a bit nearer,
> then stoppin', proddin' its ol' ears back. An' the ol' bitch
> stood there with her tail out straight. An' at the finish, he
> said, this ol' fox went right up to her and jumped on her
> side, an' she never moved, an' then the ol' fox turned
> round and went behind her, an' he said that's where they
> was for a quarter of an hour or twenty minutes. But she
> only had three puppies though; he kept one for his self,
> but it weren't no good because where the bitch went,
> that'd went. But do you know that wouldn't even bark.
> That wouldn't do nothing, not by itself, it used to keep
> with her all the time.

To me this story has the ring of truth, but when I have
mentioned it to assorted scientists, opinions are divided.
Some have even suggested that the "chromosome count" of
the fox and dog are different and so they cannot breed. I do
not believe these experts; mainly because, quite unscien-
tifically, I do not want to.

It is strange that, despite the similarities, dogs dislike
foxes so much. It is not new, for Oliver Goldsmith wrote:

> As the fox makes war upon all animals, so all others seem
> to make war upon him. The dog hunts him with peculiar

acrimony; the wolf is still a greater and more necessitous enemy, who pursues him to his very retreat. Some pretend to say that, to keep the wolf away, the fox lays at the mouth of its kennel a certain herb, to which the wolf has a particular aversion.

Like all the others, our present batch of dogs dislike foxes, and if released when the eyes of a fox reflect back in torchlight, they rush about searching for scent, bristling and growling. When they see one out in the fields, they immediately set off in pursuit, but the fox is always too quick and clever, and soon loses them.

Bramble, being a lurcher, is the traditional poaching dog of the gypsies and is supposed to run down game in silence. Whenever he sets off after a fox he is most unlurcher-like, for although he is very fast, he yaps in excitement as he runs. A few weeks ago he actually overtook a fox, and then proceeded to run alongside the surprised animal, looking at it with displeasure and yapping furiously. Running side by side, but out of biting range, they were almost the same size, but as soon as the fox reached a hedgerow, he was gone, leaving Bramble searching and confused.

The most amusing hunt came when I had three of the farm's four dogs with me; Bramble, Ben, my father's hooligan and highly-strung border collie, and Rinty, my mother's large, water-loving black labrador. We were walking along the side of the brook; Ben and Rinty went on ahead, but Bramble stopped by an old pollarded willow. He stood up on his hind legs, looking and smelling into the branches. It was March, and I assumed that he had located a mallard sitting on eggs, and went to check the tree. As I gripped a crack in the hollow trunk, to climb, I had a shock, for just as my hand went in, a fox looked out.

The other two dogs returned and bedlam broke out; the fox with its usual exit blocked, jumped, and from a height of ten feet did a spectacular belly-flop into the brook. It was the first time I had seen a fox swim. Rinty and Ben piled in after it, while Bramble, who hates water, thought momentarily;

the fox was away, so he jumped, clearing the water completely, yapping as he went. He quickly overtook the other two dogs, but as soon as the fox reached a ditch with a hedge, the unorthodox hunt was over, leaving the dogs baffled and the fox gone.

Now, every time we pass the willow Bramble stops and looks upwards expectantly. He should remember: "A fox is not taken twice in the same snare."

It is the dogs' dislike of foxes that led to one of the saddest times we have had on the farm. The collie at the time was Foss, an affectionate, friendly and intelligent dog who would let herself into the farmhouse by jumping up and striking the latch of the back door with her front paws. The other dog was Tinker, a labrador bitch, one of the best dogs we have ever had. Tinker quite literally hated foxes (except my vixen Rusty), and as soon as she scented them her hackles would rise and she would rush about in a rage snorting, as if she found their smell totally distasteful. On seeing a dead fox in a snare she dived on it and shook it as if it was an oversized rat.

A fox got its revenge one morning: I was woken up at first light by Tinker barking and straining on her chain. On looking out of my bedroom window I could see the reason, for a wild fox sat just ten yards away from her, watching quizzically as Tinker nearly choked herself with rage.

In November 1978 we were having a lot of fox trouble around the hen-houses, with attempted break-ins most nights, and rather than set snares, which we do not like using, we decided to leave Tinker loose at night. It was not a success; instead of chasing foxes, all she did was raid the dustbins of neighbours. As a result she was chained up again and Foss was left free to keep the foxes away. On the first night of her freedom I was woken up at two o'clock; she had been run over. Neighbours had found her whimpering and barking softly in the road, where she had been hit by a car and left. There was no blood but she could only move her head, and the rest of her body seemed to be completely without life. Father fetched her home in the wheelbarrow and placed her in front of the Aga to keep warm. It was sad to see, and I had to fight back the tears for we felt helpless and her eyes told of shock and fear. My sister stayed with her, but I could not get back to sleep and after an hour I got up. She cried quietly as I went to her and licked my hand; I stroked her chin and spoke to her, but still she had no movement.

Despite her injuries, her spirit remained, for next morning she growled at a cat that went too near, and she snapped at the lady vet who came to inject her. We moved her under the kitchen table and put her carefully on a sack of straw, with a blanket and a hot-water bottle for additional comfort. The vet said that movement might return and that we should wait two or three days to see what happened. We gave her tit-bits and glucose in water, and I kept imagining movement and a slight wag of her tail, but there was none. We tried to keep with her all the time, but when she was alone for just a few seconds she would whimper quietly until reassured. She could move her head perfectly, her eyes were bright and alert, and her ears responded normally. When people came she knew, her excitement showed, as if she wanted fuss, and they had to speak to her and stroke her. It was heart-rending to see, for she showed trust and fear, helplessness and hope, yet there was no real way of consoling her, or of getting her to understand her plight. It was not until the second day that we realised one of her front legs was broken, but she could feel no pain. Tinker too knew that something was wrong, and anxiety showed in her eyes.

The lady vet came again and stuck a pin in various parts of Foss's body, but there was no response. She thought that the spinal cord must have snapped and there was nothing more she could do; she said that the only recommendation she could honestly make was that Foss should be put down, and Father, with grief on his face, reluctantly agreed. I stroked her head and talked to her as the needle went in and almost as soon as blood showed in the syringe, she was dead. I had expected her to tense up, or struggle, but as I comforted her she just stopped breathing; there was no fear and her life had simply been extinguished, like the flame of a candle. It was hard to take, for she had been as one of the family, and I cried like a child, tears streaming down my face.

I carried her out and buried her under the apple trees, close to where she had often rested as I worked in the garden. It is strange how the physical act of digging helps to blunt sorrow. In the spring, ground ivy flowers beneath the blossom of the trees and we also planted some bluebell bulbs. Tinker was visibly concerned, and several times she went slowly and carefully to look into Foss's empty shed. For several days there were deep ripples of sadness on the farm, for familiar things were absent; there was no night-time barking, and the wagging tail, the bounding paws, the self-opening door, and the bright eyes wanting affection were all missing. Foxes still visited the farm at night and now, a small patch of bluebells flower every spring.

7

The Fox as a Friend

Even before I had seen a wild fox, my fascination for them had made me want a cub as a pet. Pets were always part of our life on the farm and included dogs, cats, hamsters, wild rabbits, jackdaws and a tawny owl. It seemed only logical that a fox cub should join the family. Once I had seen a fox, my longing became even greater, and when the earth in our large field was obviously occupied, I persuaded Father to dig out a cub. We went with Tom, from the High Street, and brother John, carrying a sack, a gun and two spades. John and I were both excited; we had a cage and bowls of food all ready, and told our friends of the pet we intended to capture.

Arriving at the holes we were dismayed; it was obvious that somebody had been there before us, for foxes have more than guns, traps, snares, dogs and poison to contend with. The "earth" had not been dug, instead its two entrances had been sealed, as had several rabbit holes. Tom cleared some of the soil away, and just inside found white powder and the pungent smell of gas. It seemed that we had arrived too late, but as the gas was recent, Father and Tom agreed that the young might still be alive. Looking into the hole they guessed where to dig, hoping to reach the end of the earth before the gas. They estimated exactly right and quickly dug through the roof where the earth ended, and there, with their noses pressed to the wall at the furthest point from the entrance and the creeping smell of gas, were three small cubs huddled together; but we had lost the race for they were all dead, with the one at the bottom still warm.

Because of this we never had a fox, although my regard for them remained, as did my habit of wandering through the meadows, alone, with the dog, or with a companion, always hoping for another fleeting glimpse of fox. In April 1965, the chance came that I had wanted years earlier, for when strolling through an overgrown field with a friend, the Sunday before Easter, a fox, disturbed by our voices, startled us by jumping from a hole in the trunk of an old elm, some eight feet from the ground. It was the first time I had seen a fox in a tree, and I climbed up to the hole, which was dark and fusty, but I could see nothing inside. Just as I was about to jump down, Chris, who was looking through a connecting crack lower down, noticed movement. Looking in again I too saw signs of life through the gloom and, disappearing head first into the hole I felt fur and brought out three dark cubs, covered with soft woolly hair, their eyes were still shut and their ears curled up; they looked more like alsatian puppies than foxes. One we kept, naming him Cassius, and two we put back inside. By the next day, the vixen had moved them to a less accessible home.

Difficulties immediately set in, for unlike the rabbits years earlier, we could not get the young cub to feed from a fountain-pen filler. Instead, with much embarrassment, I had to purchase a "Baby Dolly Set", from a large shop, which included a small rolling pin and a plastic potty, just to get a feeding bottle that he would accept. He quickly took to it, gulping down the sweetened milk greedily. His blue-grey eyes gradually opened, his ears uncurled, and the only problem to remain was constipation that set in with his change of diet. That too, was eventually solved by occasionally lacing his milk with syrup of figs.

Our labrador, the first Rinty, tolerated the new arrival patiently, allowing his paws to be chewed and his tail pulled, and when he died tragically, after eating half a bucket of slug bait, Cassius and the new puppy played together as if they were from the same litter. Normally the cub would stay in the garden, but twice he wandered over the road into a nearby field where he got lost in the growing corn. Both times, as Mother called him, a ripple appeared far off among the green stems and a frail whimper gradually moved towards her until he greeted her with obvious delight.

David Hosking and Chancy, a pet fox aged six months.

As he grew older his eyes became a deep brown and he was instantly attracted by all movement; leaves swaying in the wind; bees flying from flower to flower; cats, which he would attack playfully, brush first to avoid their claws, and inevitably, hens. Hens seemed almost to hypnotise him, and while they were much larger than he was, he would stalk them in the hen run, always maintaining a respectful distance. By the time he was half-grown, they seemed less intimidating, and after stalking one moulting fowl for half an hour, he finally pounced, seizing the startled bird by the tail. The hen squawked in alarm and tried to run, dragging Cassius reluctantly behind; suddenly release came, the hen was free, and Cassius was left, looking confused, with a mouthful of feathers.

He learnt quickly after that, and the next time he attacked he made no mistake, holding a hen by the neck. This meant that whenever he was not being watched over, he had to be chained up and released in the evenings when he and the puppy would chase over the lawns and garden. Although we failed to house-train him, he was allowed into the living room quite often, where he developed a keen liking for sponge cake, chocolate and hazel nuts. If none were given to him he would search the room, jumping on to the sideboard from a standing position, and landing so lightly on all fours that no ornament would be knocked over and no scratch would be made on the polished wood. On walks he always avoided water; when pheasants were flushed he would try to leap into the air in pursuit, and he enjoyed sniffing large thistles, in much the same way as dogs smell lamp posts.

But however we handled him, fussed him, and had him in the house, we could not curb his liking for ducks, and hens, and several summer mornings we woke to the cries of fowl in distress. Then, as pyjama and wellington boot clad figures chased him through the dew-soaked grass and horseradish, he skipped and danced ahead, always just out of reach, completely enjoying himself. When this happened we had to let the puppy out too, for he also enjoyed these early morning games, catching Cassius by the brush and holding

A Fox's Tale

Cassius at ten days.

Cassius explores.

Cassius finds a kitten.

Cassius plays with a patient old Rinty.

Cassius and new Rinty as friends.

Cassius dreams of hens.

him until we could make him secure once more. If pulled
from a hen he was eating, he would squeal angrily, sounding
like a pig, and once he ripped my finger open in rage, but
normally he only killed for the pleasure of seeing feathers
flutter. By the autumn he had killed so many hens that I
wrote out a small cheque for Father as conscience money.

Sadly, like the pets of childhood, his end came sooner
than anticipated, for as the mating calls of wild foxes could
be heard at night, coming from the direction of a small
spinney and the brook, he became increasingly restless,
sniffing the air and wanting to be free. One night he broke
loose again, dragging his chain behind him and disappearing completely. The following day I walked along the
hedgerows of the brook meadows calling his name, but we
saw him no more. He ran free for several miles, so we were
told later, and after a light fall of snow a farmer followed
strange tracks, as if an animal had been trailing an illegal gin
trap, which led to a shallow hole among the roots of a tree.
Not knowing what had caused them he put the barrel of his
twelve bore into the hole and pulled the trigger.

My next fox arrived unexpectedly, in 1970, when I had just
started trying to write for my living. It was an enjoyable but
uncertain time; typing with three fingers in the mornings
and then helping out on the farm when required. One good
aspect of self-employment meant that I could satisfy one of
my obsessions, local football, by playing during the week as
well as on Saturdays. At that time I kept a diary and the
arrival of the cub is duly recorded. It is interesting too, for it
shows that hares were then still plentiful about the fields,
but now, sadly, they are seldom seen. The week started in a
pleasant way:

Sunday April 19th
A most memorable walk. It was dry but the wind was cool.
Over on some ploughed land Tinker put up a fox which ran
off without much fuss and quickly lost her. It looked as if it
usually lays up in the middle of the field, as a small area of

soil was quite worn. Tinker also put up a hare and pheasants. There was a very small amount of frogspawn in the pond and a warbler in some blackthorn – the same place as last year. Some yellow wagtails were in the grass.

Monday 20th
The Fordson developed a leak and so we can only use one tractor on the land now that land-work has started.

Tuesday 21st
Fordson still out of action.

A woman rang up stating that she had a fox cub and asking if I would like to rear it. I will pick it up tomorrow.

Wednesday 22nd
I picked up the cub in the morning. The woman found it bedraggled and deserted in a ditch. It is absolutely beautiful and looks to be about a month old. The lady could not cope with it as she has two Jack Russell terriers. I put him in an ancient trunk with wire over it. Dad was going to put his old farm papers in it. If he does they will have an interesting odour when he comes to read them.

The cub makes more noise than Cassius used to and we decided to call him Claudius. On seeing Tinker, he wagged his tail, put his ears down, and made shrill noises of excitement. Tinker was not impressed and we will have to be very strict with her. In the afternoon I went on the back of the drill to finish putting the oats in. Ellen [my sister-in-law] brought coffee and a bar of chocolate. There is something very pleasant about drilling; a sense of both challenge and hope.

A wheatear arrived near us. It is several years since I have seen one pass through.

Thursday 23rd
Still only one tractor and John spent the day spring-tine harrowing. Played football in the afternoon and scored three. The second was another dipping volley.

Claudius is settling down well and is full of life. Tinker snapped at him and I hit her hard; I hope she has learned her lesson. I try to make sure that she still gets a lot of fuss so that she does not get jealous.

Claudius has a good appetite but does not keep his mind on it long enough. His favourite place is under the grand-father clock or in the hole near the fire. [A small brick construction near the large open fireplace; nobody has yet been able to say what it was once used for. The farmhouse was built in about 1470.]

Friday 24th
Went drilling with John again. Barley this time, and despite the threatening weather we managed to finish all right. We saw one of the leverets that he caught the other day. It looks as if the other has been killed. The wheatear came quite close and Ellen once more supplied coffee and cake.

As soon as I got home I took out Claudius. He was hungry, lively and extremely well. Tinker appeared to have accepted him. Mum gave Tinker a mutton bone and Claudius a small piece of meat. The cub finished his quickly and then ran off to sniff the bone. Tinker chopped him once – quickly and without fuss and he reeled over dead, just by the mat near the back door. Blood poured out of his mouth. I picked him up but it was clear that he was already dead. Blood dripped all over the carpet and the stone tiles. It was so sad. One second full of vitality and a delight to watch and hold, the next nothing, a helpless heap of fur, still with the light in his eyes but blood on his nose and mouth. I was very upset but I could not really blame Tinker.

My final fox, Rusty, a vixen, arrived already fully grown. By then my sister Rachael was nursing in Northampton and friends of hers had found Rusty as a cub, but by the time the young fox had grown up into an attractive vixen, she had outgrown her accommodation and they could not cope with her. I collected her in an empty tea chest, covered with wire, and brought her back to the farm in the car.

At first she was frightened, nervous and suspicious, but gradually her fear subsided and she came to accept me as a friend. Other members of the family too, she accepted, but when any strangers visited, she would disappear under her box and would rarely come out. Even Tinker tolerated the affectionate little vixen, and they would greet each other with wagging tails. At the call of "Rusty, Rusty", Foss would rush up to the run and tear round and round, making a well worn track. Occasionally I would let her in to play, but I had to be careful, for a fox is smaller and much more delicate than an exuberant border collie.

The run was made from chain-link fencing, with some of the wire buried, as she loved digging. It had a wire roof too because of her agility and her inevitable liking for hens. Even in captivity her speed was astonishing and when a blackbird foolishly flew into her run, she caught it in mid-air. Wandering mice, rats, birds and a half-grown hedgehog all met a similar swift end.

Sadly, we could not have Rusty in the house, for in the early days as soon as she came in, as a matter of course, she would relieve herself on the doormat and the aroma would linger in the living room for days. Because of this I would often play with her in her run; she would chase her tail, dive on a ball, like a wild fox with a mouse, and when given a real mouse, caught in a trap, she would go wild with delight. She would dive on it, rush around her run and then fling it about in all directions. Finally, tired, she would sit down and eat her toy. Like Cassius before her, she hated water, but she was a dainty, delicate eater. Her favourite tit-bit, apart from raw hens, were giblets of hen, pheasant or duck, dripping with gravy.

Whenever I went to her she would wag her brush vigorously, with her ears flat, making a variety of friendly whines and whimpers. Often she would jump on my shoulders and rub her chin and nose through my hair. It was a habit she seemed to enjoy. One evening when I had planned to go out, I went to play with her before I left. As usual she jumped on my shoulders and rubbed my hair with her chin. Suddenly

Rusty looking crafty.

my head felt warm; it was a strange feeling and I touched my hair – it was dripping. Rusty had kindly relieved herself on my head; I stayed at home for more than one evening and smelt like a fox for three days. Harriet, who at the age of 86 still comes to help clean my cottage one morning a week, thought Rusty's performance was a great joke: "She knew what she was doing; she knew your hair needed a wash." Harriet likes foxes and in her childhood did not have a rocking-horse, but a rocking-fox.

Occasionally, and out of character, Rusty would be unresponsive, clearly wanting her freedom; when that happened she would make a peculiar high-pitched screaming noise, sounding almost exactly like a squealing pig. Several times I was tempted to release her, but a fox that has lost some of its fear of man and dogs would not last very long in the wild.

For a few months Rusty had company in her run, as I was given a small cub called Sidney. He had been dug out of an earth, but his life had been spared and he was offered to me. I accepted him, as Rusty needed a companion, and one day, although it is said that foxes can be very difficult to breed in captivity, I hoped they would mate. Whereas the vixen was quite small, Sidney grew into a fine dog fox, alert, greedy, and playful, with a large brush, and a soft thick coat. Unlike Rusty he was a complete glutton and at feeding time he would stuff his jaws to bursting point, carry the food to a safe place, then without eating it he would quickly return for more. Unlike both Cassius and Rusty he enjoyed water, and everything that moved he chased, including bumble bees; those he caught in his mouth he chewed and swallowed with obvious enjoyment.

Unfortunately the attempt to get Rusty and Sidney to breed did not take place, for as the breeding season approached, he escaped, and sadly he did not return. It is strange, that although Tinker accepted the pet foxes, she continued to hate all wild foxes. One bout of barking was quite justified, for three pairs of eyes reflected back in the beam of my lantern. After another outburst I let her off her chain and she trapped a full-grown fox beneath a slightly raised hen-house which was just high enough to allow a fox to crawl under, but just low enough to keep a dog at bay. I got the rifle from the house and decided reluctantly that I had to shoot it. I lay on the ground in my pyjamas with the fox completely exposed in torchlight, and its head lined up in the sights. Just as I was going to pull the trigger it moved and I noticed that it was wearing a collar; it was Sidney. I could not shoot, called Tinker away and let him go; he had a lucky escape.

After the departure of Sidney I considered staking Rusty out at night during January, to see if she would mate with a wild fox. But on reflection it seemed too dangerous, as it would have left her vulnerable to roaming dogs. By coincidence I then discovered two more tame foxes in the next village. They were fine animals, well looked after, and fed on a diet of frozen rats; they were found as cubs in Wales and rescued from motorway construction. The dog was large and placid, named Botoch, the Gaelic for old man, and the vixen was more temperamental and called Creoch, or thief. When Rusty was introduced into their cage it was not known how they would react, for foxes, like most animals are very territorial.

At first, whenever Rusty approached either of the other two, their ears would go flat and back, and with their mouths open they would make strange threatening noises, like a cross between a growl and a squeal, almost coughed out. On one occasion Rusty was bitten sharply across the nose by the other vixen, but in the main they were just threats. Another time, Botoch arched his back, and with his brush aloft, he rubbed against the wire mesh as if he was scenting to assert his authority, but then he disappeared inside his box. Rusty spent most of her time under a sawn-up section of hollow tree trunk, but gradually the swearing and displaying declined, until by the end of the month they were all living together quite peacefully. Rusty and Botoch even slept together, but unfortunately they did nothing more than sleep. On returning to the farm, she was very excited and pulled so hard on her lead that I let her go. She ran straight back to her shed and wagged her brush, wanting to play. The stay had not unsettled her, but neither had it given her cubs.

In winter Rusty stayed in her shed, with plenty of straw; she could see out and play, but to give her more exercise and interest, I sometimes took her for a walk around the fields on her lead. She would pull all the way, and like Cassius, was totally oblivious to all commands. During a freeze we walked on to the frozen brook; the smell of voles in the bank excited her and she dug frantically in the snow. Wild foxes too had used the frozen brook as an easy way to get about, for fox droppings were on the ice as well as distinctive fox tracks, as foxes put one foot almost directly in front of another. In summer she would go to her outside run, which she enjoyed; digging, running, with Foss one side of the wire, and her the other, sunbathing and playing. But inevitably she sometimes became bored and when she did, she often tried to escape. Her first spell of freedom lasted over a day and she returned squealing and wagging her brush. The second time she was out only a minute; as Rachael went in to her shed to feed her, Rusty rushed out. She ran straight up to a hen, seized it by the neck and immediately dragged it back to her shed, dead.

As she got older, she would stay away longer. Each time she went, I would walk along the hedgerows, with the dogs, calling her name, but she would never return until she wanted to. She returned one night quite unexpectedly; it was bright and moonlit and I was checking the cattle yard at 11.00 p.m. Suddenly she was at my feet, whining and wagging her brush before rolling over to have her stomach rubbed.

On another occasion she was away for four or five days and I had given up any hope of her returning. On that occasion she emerged from thick brambles in the brook meadows and greeted the dogs like long lost friends before running over to me. She was in fine condition and had obviously been living well.

Her final escape came in April 1979. Following some peculiar mental aberration, I was fighting the general election in London, contesting a seat I could not win, to get a new view of politics. Her escape was more important to me than political campaigning, and ten days after returning home to play football, I again returned home to look for Rusty. For two days I went with the dogs around the hedgerows, calling her name without success, and on the Monday I reluctantly and sadly returned to London. The following day her body was found in the next parish; she was hardly marked, but her neck was broken, as if she had approached a large dog – at least it was a relief to know that she had not suffered in a trap or with shotgun wounds. She had been part of the family for nine years and her loss was deeply felt; she was buried next to Foss under the apple trees.

I would not want to keep another fox, for in retrospect it is unfair to them, as they lose some of their fear and it is fear that is so important for their survival in the wild; I would rather see them free. However, I have no regrets about my foxes; they were all beautiful creatures and I enjoyed learning from them. It was a privilege and a pleasure to share their lives on the farm, and who knows, the spirit of Sidney could still be alive and well in the hedgerows, and peering with anticipation into the hen-houses.

8

The Fox in the Field

Inevitably, in any book about the fox, mention has to be made of hunting, for the two are inexorably linked, and have been for centuries. Consequently, I was going to call this chapter "The Fox as a Fiend", but after a few minutes thought it became clear that few fox-hunters regard the fox as a fiend; they are in the strange and ambiguous position of actually liking the fox. Their feelings are summed up best by Jorrocks, that wonderful overweight hunting grocer created by R. S. Surtees in 1843:

> Oh, how that beautiful word, Fox, gladdens my 'eart, and warms the declinin' embers of my age. The 'oss and the 'ound were made for each other, and nature threw in the Fox as a connectin' link between the two. He's perfect

A fox hunt as depicted in a Bewick woodcut of 1806.

symmetry, and my affection for him is a perfect paradox. In the summer I loves him with all the hardour of affection; not an 'air of his beautiful 'ead would I hurt; the sight of him is more glorious nor the Lord Mayor's show! But when the hautumn comes – when the brownin' copse and cracklin' stubble proclaim the farmer's fears are past, then, dash my vig, 'ow I glories in pursuin' of him to destruction, and holdin' him above the bayin' pack!

And yet [added Mr. Jorrocks thoughtfully], it ar'nt that I loves the fox less, but that I loves the 'ound more.

In his *Memoirs of a Fox-Hunting Man* (1928), Siegfried Sassoon shows that he too did not regard the fox as his enemy. He was on his second hunt when:

Something rustled the dead leaves; not more than ten yards from where we stood, a small russet animal stole out on to the path and stopped for a photographic instant to take a look at us. It was the first time I had ever seen a fox, though I have seen a great many since – both alive and dead. By the time he had slipped out of sight again I had just begun to realise what it was that had looked at me with such human alertness. Why I should have behaved as I did I will not attempt to explain, but when Denis stood up in his stirrups and emitted a shrill "Huick-holler," I felt spontaneously alarmed for the future of the fox. "Don't do that; they'll catch him!" I exclaimed.

The old Duke of York wrote about other attractions of hunting in *The Master of Game*:

Hunters live more joyfully than any other men. For when the hunter riseth in the morning, and he sees a sweet fair morn and clear weather and bright, and he heareth the song of the small birds, the which sing so sweetly with great melody and full of love each in its own language in the best wise that it can according that it learneth of its own kind. And when the sun is arisen, he shall see fresh

The hunter's affection for the fox is clear to see. H. Chandler, the Garth Huntsman, with his tame fox of 1907.

dew upon the small twigs and grasses, and the sun by his
virtue shall make them shine. And that is the great joy and
liking to the hunter's heart.

But whether hunting is supported or opposed, whether it
continues or becomes banned, it has to be admitted that it
has become a traditional part of the English countryside.
Aesthetically, to see hounds, horses and riders streaming
over an autumn or winter landscape makes a stirring and
unforgettable sight. To Jorrocks it was a total obsession:
"'Unting is all that's worth living for – all time is lost wot is
not spent in 'unting – it is like the hair we breathe – if we
have it not we die – it's the sport of kings, the image of war
without its guilt, and only five and twenty per cent of its
danger."

Even his wife suffered from his love of hounds: "'Unting
fills my thoughts by day, and many a good run I have in my
sleep. Many a dig in the ribs I gives Mrs. J. when I think
they're running into the warmint. No man is fit to be called a
sportsman wot doesn't kick his wife out of bed on a haverage
once in three weeks."

After a hunt, then he enjoyed remembering the day's
events. Indeed Surtees gives one scene a classic line, when
Jorrocks and a companion are sitting in front of the fire, in
the dark, Jorrocks asks Pigg to: "Look out the winder,
James, and see wot 'un a night it is." Pigg answered:
"Hellish dark, and smells of cheese" – he had opened the
wrong door and gone into the pantry.

Surtees created some fine characters in all his books and
his descriptions and conversations contain much remark-
ably accurate social comment and parody. At a hunt ball a
character says scornfully: "These sorts of boobies think that
people come to balls to do nothing but dance: whereas
everyone knows that the real business of a ball is either to
look out for a wife, to look after a wife, or to look after
somebody else's wife."

It is a fact that hunting, horsey people seem to be attracted
to other hunting, horsey people, therefore another eccentric

gentleman, Mr. Sponge, comments; "Women never look so well as when one comes in wet and dirty from hunting." The women are even measured in "hands" like horses: "I hate a weedy woman – fifteen two and a half – that's to say, five feet four's plenty of height for a woman."

Walter de la Mare could well have been inspired by Surtees and the world of Jorrocks when he wrote "The Huntsmen":

> Three jolly gentlemen,
> In coats of red,
> Rode their horses
> Up to bed.
>
> Three jolly gentlemen,
> Snored till morn,
> Their horses champing
> The golden corn.
>
> Three jolly gentlemen,
> At break of day,
> Came clitter-clatter down the stairs
> And galloped away.

Today, huntsmen are often seen in a very different light, hence:

> A huntsman one day confided,
> That by pomp he always was guided.
> Then he fell off his horse,
> With exceeding great force;
> In other words he was de-rided.

Walter de la Mare wrote another quite short poem simply called "The Hunt":

> Tallyho! Tallyho! –
> Echo faints far astray,
> On the still, misty air,
> And the Hunt is away!

Horsemen and hounds
Stream over the hill;
And, brush well behind him,
Pelts with a will
Old Reynard the Fox –
As in conscience he may,
For hot at his heels
Sweep Trim, Trap and Tray;
Chestnut, and black
And flea-bitten grey
But the Crafty One knows
Every inch of the way!
Thicket and Spinney,
Gully and dell,
Where the stream runs deep,
And the otters dwell –
Hemlock, garlic,
Bog asphodel –
He'll lead them a dance,
Though they ride like hell.
And – wily old animal,
Cunning as they! –
He'll live – to go hunting –
Another fine day.

It seems inevitable that at the end of the poem the fox gets away, as it does in nearly all the stories and poems involving a hunt. One of the best fox stories ever written was published in 1939 – *Wild Lone* by "BB", and beautifully illustrated by the author, under his actual name of Denys Watkins-Pitchford. In the original manuscript the book ends with the fox, Rufus, dying of heart failure after a long hunt, but the publishers thought it was too sad and "BB" changed his ending:

It is quiet now in the kennels save for the whimper of sleeping hounds or the rustle of straw on the benches as a dream-ridden leg thrusts spasmodically.

It is quiet also in the stables and in the dwellings of mankind. Strange this stilling of movement, this closing of eyes! Magical slumber, magical silences!

Such a short while ago these actors in the past drama were afire with movement and life.

Where now the blackbirds that ran upon the lawn before the windows of Wildwoods, where the rooks, busy among the fruitful oak branches by the leaf-strewn pond?

Even the great cities are strangely muted and dimmed, the humming in the hive is low.

There is a waiting for the light, for the sun again. The birds and animals sleep as insects sleep in the chinks of a wintry tree, and even the astonishing brain of man comes under this magic spell, and reason yaws like a rudderless ship among the troubled seas of dreams.

The Huntsman sleeps, on his back and snoring; the whipper-in is busy with foxy phantoms, muttering to himself.

Buried deep within many walls the Master sleeps, and only a mouse is awake in his dressing room, gnawing the woodwork under a wardrobe.

Old Bumpus, in flannel night-shirt, is playing a steady solo on the nosoon, an alarm clock to keep him monotonous company.

Under the cold sky and keen sweet airs the dark hump of Hieaway is still breathing; it seems that even the trees are dreaming.

Yet there is one that sleepeth not.

See! A shadow comes stealing from the skirts of the firs and goes, noiselessly, down into the valley fields, limping slightly with the old limp, one ear erect like a shark's fin.

May the good earth keep you, now and for always! Good hunting, little red fox, and . . . good-bye!

A more recent book, *The Belstone Fox* (1970), has a novel twist at the end of the story, for it is not the fox that dies but the huntsman. In the main, it is a happy story about a fox called Tag, that was brought up with Merlin, a young fox-hound. Later on, Merlin found himself hunting his one-time companion:

Tag had the devil in him – the game had slowed down to the point where it had become boring, so now he was going to liven it up a little . . . he ran down the hill with his brush streaming out behind him, straight towards the oncoming hounds.

It was Merlin who saw him, as the fox rocketed past only thirty yards away, going in the opposite direction. Because they were hunting a failing line, the hounds were concentrating hard on their noses and would possibly not have noticed a double-decker bus going by, but something made Merlin look up . . . with a whimper of excitement he swung round and went after Tag as fast as he could.

From one field away, Asher [the huntsman] watched as Tag flew past the labouring pack, holding his breath as he waited for them to see the young fox, but only one hound turned and sprinted after him. With an overwhelming sense of disbelief, Asher saw Tag turn and run back towards his old friend – saw the foxhound and the fox meet and whirl in an ecstasy of delight, capering and dancing in the middle of the field in which he stood like a statue, while the rest of the pack toiled on up the hill, away from them.

It didn't last for long . . . old Affable, who was well towards the rear, caught a whiff of Tag's new line, for it was being blown diagonally across the hillside by the east wind. She swung and spoke to it, breathing it in eagerly and giving tongue in a series of excited yelps. The rest of

The fox in the snow.

The adaptability of the fox is well known and a bench at night provides a surprising vantage place.

the pack turned and came back to her, and within seconds they were tearing back down the hill on a breast-high scent.

The author, David Rook, has a more pleasant way of writing about scent than the early Duke of York; he wrote: "The hunting for a fox is fair for the good cry of the hounds that follow him so nigh and with so good will. Always the scent of him, for he flies through the thick wood and also he stinketh evermore."

Gradually Tag in *The Belstone Fox*, turned into a legend and his antics were reported in the fictitious magazine *The Hunt*:

Three seasons ago, towards the end of the cub-hunting period, a young dog-fox with a vivid white streak above his left eye gave hounds a short run from Hungarton wood before scent gave out. This was the first known appearance of the now famous Belstone Fox. Later in the season they hunted him again, having changed on to him from a tired fox, and proceeded to chalk up one of the best runs of the season. Once again he gave them the slip, and the legend was born. Were it not for the clear identification mark on his mask, it would be logical to ascribe the exploits of this one fox to a dozen or so, but he has been seen too often and by too many people to doubt the legend any longer.

These are the facts: he was hunted three more times that season, once from Hungarton and twice from distant coverts. Two of these hunts were short and sharp, but the third was memorable, with a point of twelve miles and about seventeen as hounds ran. After a long report in *Hunting Today*, he acquired the sobriquet of "The Belstone Fox" and his fame began to spread beyond the boundaries of the Hunt . . .

On one occasion, for example, Smith [Asher Smith] clearly saw him running across the backs of a tightly packed flock of sheep; when the sheep broke up and started to run, the fox maintained his place on the back of one of them while it ran for fifty yards or so, and then jumped to the ground, or was shaken off.

Another characteristic of this fox is his apparent familiarity with the appurtenances of what we in the country call "progress". He has, on many occasions, made a wide detour in order to run through the gardens in front of a row of houses, and twice has been seen to run into a house through an open back door, leaving via an open window at the front! This must sound like fiction, but the instances are well authenticated, and identification is fool-proof.

Another story, not quite so easy to verify, is that he jumped up into the back of a slow moving Mini-van and was driven away from the scene of the hunt . . .

When you consider the number of times per season that this fox is hunted, and when you then consider the

The fox's resourcefulness when pursued is legendary. "Any Port in a Storm" from the Illustrated Sporting and Dramatic News *of February 1884 shows how it's done.*

unorthodox situations in which he is "found", you begin to wonder exactly who is finding whom. One or two examples will explain my point – and both, definitely, are true. The first occurred when hounds were drawing Burnetts Wood one morning in December '65. They were in the process of drawing it blank when the field were startled to see a handsome dog fox appear over the sky-line and trot calmly past them – not more than fifty yards away – and into the covert. It was, of course, our friend. One minute later, hounds "found" him and an enjoyable hunt ensued.

The second example which must surely be some sort of record, was when our fox actually turned up at the Meet. It happened at the village of Scarford in February of this year, when hounds were meeting on the green. About eighty people had turned up mounted, and a good number of foot-and-car followers as well, when someone noticed that the fox was sitting on a nearby wall, surveying the scene with great interest and evident enjoyment!

Now the implication of these two occurrences, and of many others, is inescapable; it is that the Belstone Fox actually "finds" the hounds, rather than vice versa. In short, if they don't go looking for him, he goes out looking for them.

The book was made into a successful film; it was interesting to note how in every scene involving an actor and the fox, the person concerned held Tag, suggesting that the fox was as unresponsive to training as Rusty and Cassius had been with me.

One of the most remarkable descriptions of a fox hunt is to be found in John Masefield's long and exceptional narrative poem – *Reynard the Fox, or the Ghost Heath Run*. He did not like hunting, but it is also clear that he understood it, he enjoyed the wide range of characters that took part in it and he had a sensitive and appreciative view of the English countryside. All three elements are shown in his description of the "whip" – Tom Dansey:

He was a small, lean, wiry man
With sunk cheeks weathered to a tan
Scarred by the spikes of hawthorn sprays
Dashed thro', head down, on going days,
In haste to see the line they took.
There was a beauty in his look
It was intent. His speech was plain.
Marron's head, reaching to the rein,
Had half his thought before he spoke.
His "gone away" when foxes broke,
Was like a bell. His chief delight
Was hunting fox from noon to night.
His pleasure lay in hounds and horses,
He loved the Seven Springs water-courses,
Those flashing brooks (in good sound grass,
Where scent would hang like breath on glass).
He loved the English countryside;
The wine-leaved bramble in the ride,
The lichen on the apple-trees,
The poultry ranging on the lees,
The farms, the moist earth-smelling cover,
His wife's green grave at Mitcheldover,
Where snowdrops pushed at the first thaw.
Under his hide his heart was raw
With joy and pity of these things.

Again at the conclusion of the exhausting poem, although
one fox meets its end, the fox of the chase survives to run
another day. Indeed, it has an unusually happy ending; the
hunted fox, the huntsmen and the readers are all happy and
content:

After an hour no riders came,
The day drew by like an ending game;
A robin sang from a pufft red breast,
The fox lay quiet and took his rest.
A wren on a tree-stump carolled clear,
Then the starlings wheeled in a sudden sheer,

The Fox in the Field

The rooks came home to the twiggy hive
In the elm-tree tops which the winds do drive.
Then the noise of the rooks fell slowly still,
And the lights came out in the Clench Brook Mill
Then a pheasant cocked, then an owl began
With the cry that curdles the blood of man.

The stars grew bright as the yews grew black,
The fox rose stiffly and stretched his back.
He flaired the air, then he padded out
To the valley below him dark as doubt,
Winter-thin with the young green crops,
For Old Cold Crendon and Hilcote Copse.

As he crossed the meadows at Naunton Larking,
The dogs in the town all started barking,
For with feet all bloody and flanks all foam,
The hounds and the hunt were limping home;
Limping home in the dark, dead beaten,
The hounds all rank from a fox they'd eaten,
Dansey saying to Robin Dawe.
"The fastest and longest I ever saw."
And Robin answered, "O Tom, 'twas good,
I thought they'd changed in the Mourne End Wood,
But now I feel that they did not change.
We've had a run that was great and strange;
And to kill in the end, at dusk, on grass.
We'll turn to the back and take a glass;
For the hounds, poor souls, are past their forces.
And a gallon of ale for our poor horses,
And some bits of bread for the hounds, poor things,
After all they've done (for they've done like kings)
Would keep them going till we get in.
We had it alone from Nun's Wood Whin."
Then Tom replied, "If they changed or not,
There've been few runs longer and none more hot,
We shall talk of to-day until we die."

The stars grew bright in the winter sky,
The wind came keen with a tang of frost,
The brook was troubled for new things lost,
The copse was happy for old things found,
The fox came home and he went to ground.

And the hunt came home and the hounds were fed,
They climbed to their bench and went to bed,
The horses in stable loved their straw.
"Good-night, my beauties," said Robin Dawe.

Then the moon came quiet and flooded full
Light and beauty on clouds of wool,
On a feasted fox at rest from hunting,
In the beech wood grey where the brocks were grunting.

The beech wood grey rose dim in the night
With moonlight fallen in pools of light,
The long dead leaves on the ground were rimed.
A clock struck twelve and the church-bells chimed.

I have hunted twice; the first time was for a book I was
writing – *The Hunter and the Hunted*. I thought it only fair,
that if I was to write a book mentioning hunting, I should
learn to ride and follow hounds. Then I would see what
really happened for myself, and not rely on the views of
those who are actively "pro" or "anti". Specifically for that
purpose I learnt to ride, or more accurately, hang on – a long
and painful process, for riding is far more difficult than it
appears when being done by experts. I quickly had a fall, but
it was not from the horse, as expected, but from my bike. For
dressed in a smart new riding hat and boots purchased from
Moss Bros, and clutching a crop, I somehow managed to
ride into the verge and headlong to the ground, in full view
of the stables and my riding teacher.

The first hunt was memorable; held on Christmas Eve in
my home county of Cambridgeshire. I was on a hired horse
that, when I was learning, was slow and uninterested: but as

soon as it saw the hounds and other horses it became alert and frisky. It was an exciting day:

> Suddenly the hounds started up in full cry, and Jason [my horse] seemed to boil. We were off again, another fox had been flushed from the hole and this time the hunt was really on; one large horse refused at the small fence, almost throwing its rider into the mire, but Jason jumped it with no hesitation and we were immediately galloping furiously. The sun came out as the late morning cloud melted away, catching the colours, the movement, and the sleek coats of the horses. The hounds streamed out along the edge of the ploughland, still in full cry and we followed, well to the fore. We ran in a wide arc, round some farm buildings and out onto the road, to gallop along the verge, away from the village and past the mill; the grey-haired man was still taking photographs and his daughter held a banner proclaiming "Ban Hunting"; he obviously objected to the hunt being anywhere near his plot of twenty acres, with its small grassfields, cattle and sheep.
>
> The hounds turned into a large field of winter wheat, running fast and steadily. Jason was going well, although the ground was very heavy, and he cleared several ditches easily and eagerly: some were narrow and shallow, and others were wide and cavernous. We followed a ditch onto stubble, still galloping hard. The sun was in my eyes but I could see that far from tiring, Jason was actually looking for the hounds. I was sweating, but having taken the advice of several old men who had dealt with military horses and ridden in earlier days – "keep your knees in and your heels down" – I had experienced no difficulty in staying on; but still the hooves pounded, water squelched, mud flew, and the wind cut into and cooled my cheeks.

The actual hunt lasted sixty-five minutes of almost non-stop galloping. In that time the fox ran in a large circle and tried to lose its scent in a typical way – it ran deliberately through a flock of sheep. For me the hunt finished as I had wanted it to, with the fox taking safe refuge down a large badger sett. I will always remember the end of the day:

The hounds and a greatly reduced number of riders moved off to begin another hunt, but with the sun beginning to sink I decided to ride the twelve miles back to the stables. Jason was reluctant to go, and whenever he heard the horn his ears twitched and he turned his head towards the sound. The sun was bright and warm for the time of year and the air felt fresh and clean. A low thorn hedge was still decorated as if in autumn, with clusters of copper-gilded leaves, strings of brilliant red bryony berries, and clumps of hips and haws that gave sprays of orange and crimson to the dormant winter wood. Some ridges and furrows in a field of old grassland dazzled with luminosity and even the ploughed land seemed slightly iridescent. As the sun fell in a ball of white light, the sky passed through its soothing shades of sunset and the woodland elms and oaks seemed to glow with deep purple. The moon was almost full and slowly the stars dotted the sky; close to the stables Jason lost a shoe, but it was too near home to cause concern. There was little traffic, it was still and clear, it was Christmas night, and as the horse plodded into the stable yard I was filled with an inner warmth of contentment.

The other hunt was for the *Daily Telegraph*, after I had been invited to ride with one of the top hunts in the country, the Fernie and, despite my appalling horsemanship, I accepted. The Fernie itself is one of the "shire" hunts, with much of its area down to grass, and with a reputation for fast, exciting hunting. It is important too in the history of hunting, for it is in southern Leicestershire, where fox-hunting as it is carried out today was first developed by a wealthy young country gentleman named Hugo Meynell (pronounced almost like kennel), in the late eighteenth century.

The morning of the hunt was cold and clear, with frost

lingering along the hedgerows and ditches. The meet was held at Thorpe Lubenham Hall, a large country house, surrounded by parkland, where over 150 horses and riders assembled. It was an attractive scene, aesthetically pleasing and rich in tradition. Indeed, that is one of the contributions hunting makes to the countryside, it helps to retain the feeling of rural living, despite the never-ending encroachment by plastic suburbia and pseudo-sophistication.

There were top hats, bowlers, red coats, large hunters and small ponies, as well as three women riding side-saddle. Among the riders was a former Labour member of parliament who had become a socialist Lord; he had also once been the Master of the Pytchley fox hounds. I was dressed in an old anorak and my mother's gardening trousers (ski-trousers – as they stretch ideally for gardening and, as it turned out, hunting), but his Lordship made me feel welcome. As I talked to him I nearly had my first fall of the day, for drinking the "styrup cup", a large sherry, while also holding the reins and crop, and controlling the horse, is surprisingly difficult for a novice.

As the hounds moved off it was an impressive sight, but because of the frost some riders suggested that scent would be scarce. The hounds first went along the old disused Market Harborough to Rugby railway line, where they worked in the brambles and scrub, but there were no signs of a fox. There were other interesting signs, however, for although the Fernie is a "shire" hunt, those who follow it, on horseback, in cars and on foot, represent a wide cross-section of society, from members of the old aristocracy to ordinary working people. This could be detected in the conversation, for there was a range of accents from public school and Stock Exchange to public bar and stock-yard. Clothing too, was varied, from the new and immaculate, straight from a Moss Bros window, to the holes and patches of hand-me-downs and darning needles.

After the railway line the hounds went into an area of woodland and several short hunts followed, including a longer one around the village of Loughton. At one time I found myself almost at the front, as hounds streamed over winter wheat and made for a small copse. As they went in at one end, the fox left at the other; it seemed none too concerned and went over grass, through a hedge and away. The huntsman was convinced that they know when scent is bad, "for they almost stop and look at you".

Despite the fact that the hunting was apparently poor, I enjoyed it, for there were times when I experienced the clichéd but real attractions of "the chase"; the pounding hooves, mud flying and the adrenalin flowing. There were jumps too, hedges, fences and "tiger-traps" over ditches, demanding both courage and a cool nerve. I possess neither, and despite the earlier reassurances of an old countryman who told me: "You'll be all right, they'll be packed in so tight you won't be able to fall off", I managed one "involuntary dismount" and two falls, out of seven jumps. The most embarrassing part, was getting back on, for the only way an inexperienced 5 foot 5 inch body can remount a horse 16.2 hands high is by using the nearest fence as a ladder. Each time I fell off, a famous and kindly writer cum television producer who loves hunting, hung back to make sure I was still in one piece and could resume.

Some of the hedgerows and copses were part of the old "hunting landscape", for although agriculture in Leicester-shire is well run and efficient, much of its appealing coun-tryside is dominated by features specifically left for hunting. A large number of the hedges and trees of the post-enclosure era have been retained and many of the copses and woods once drawn by Hugo Meynell and his hounds are still drawn today, benefiting many forms of wildlife in addition to the fox. As a result, whether galloping hard, falling off my horse again, or hearing the hounds and the distant huntsman's horn, I felt a peculiar sense of continuity – of being linked to the past by a living tradition.

It was a good day, ending with the frost returning – white breath, horses stamping and steaming, tiredness and satis-faction. Again all the foxes had escaped, but I still carry a memento of my day – without realising it at the time I broke the little finger on my right hand, and it is still bent today.

Since I started writing for a living I have done many interesting, even dangerous things; I have walked unarmed past lions; I have visited a war zone; been lost in mountains during a snow storm, and seen many wild and remote places. But I have to admit that hunting is as exciting as anything I have ever experienced, and all the clichés about it are exactly right. Yet there is something else that should be remembered about hunting – and that is the fox. In some rural areas foxes still have many enemies, but as long as people hunt they will ensure the preservation of their quarry. Consequently, rather than posing a threat, hunting offers the wild country fox its greatest insurance against excessive persecution. Such a conclusion may be strange, but it happens to be true.

9

The Fox's Foray

A fox jumped up one winter's night,
And begged the moon to give him light,
For he'd many miles to trot that night
Before he reached the town O!
Town O! Town O!
For he'd many miles to trot that night
Before he reached his town O!

The first place he came was a farmer's yard,
Where the ducks and geese declared it hard
That their nerves should be shaken and their rest so marred
By a visit from Mr. Fox O!
Fox O! Fox O!
That their nerves should be shaken and their rest so marred
By a visit from Mr. Fox O!

He took the grey goose by the neck,
And swung him right across his back;
The grey goose cried out, Quack, quack, quack,
With his legs hanging dangling down O!
Down O! Down O!
The grey goose cried out, Quack, quack, quack,
With his legs hanging dangling down O!

The Fox's Foray

Old Mother Slipper Slopper jumped out of bed,
And out of the window she popped her head:
Oh! John, John, John, the grey goose is gone,
And the fox is off to his den O!
Den O! Den O!
Oh! John, John, John, the grey goose is gone,
And the fox is off to his den O!

John ran up to the top of the hill,
And blew his whistle loud and shrill;
Said the fox, that is very pretty music; still –
I'd rather be in my den O!
Den O! Den O!
Said the fox, that is very pretty music; still –
I'd rather be in my den O!

The fox went back to his hungry den,
And his dear little foxes, eight, nine, ten;
Quoth they, Good daddy, you must go there again,
If you bring such good cheer from the farm O!
Farm O! Farm O!
Quoth they, Good daddy, you must go there again,
If you bring such good cheer from the farm O!

The fox and wife, without any strife,
Said they never ate a better goose in all their life:
They did very well without fork and knife,
And the little ones picked the bones O!
Bones O! Bones O!
They did very well without fork or knife,
And the little ones picked the bones O!

10

The Fox's Prophecy

1. Tom Hill was in the saddle
   One bright November morn
   The echoing glades of Guiting Wood
   Were ringing with his horn.

2. In stately march the sable rooks
   Followed the clanking plough
   Apart their watchful sentinel
   Cawed from the topmost bough.

3. Soft fleecy clouds were sailing
   Across the vault of blue
   A fairer hunting morning
   No huntsman ever knew;

4. But sound and sight of beauty
   Fell dull on eye and ear
   The huntsman's heart was heavy,
   His brow oppressed with care.

5. High in his stirrups raised, he stood
   And long he gazed around,
   And breathlessly and anxiously
   He listened for a sound.

6. No voice of hound, no sound of horn,
   The woods around were mute,
   As though the earth had swallowed up
   His comrades, man and brute.

7. He thought, "I must essay to find
   My hounds at any cost,
   A huntsman who has lost his hounds,
   Is but a huntsman lost."

8. Then round he turned his horse's head,
   And shook his bridle free,
   When he was aware of an aged fox
   That sat beneath a tree.

9. He raised his eyes in glad surprise,
   That huntsman keen and bold,
   But there was in that fox's look
   That made his blood run cold:

10. He raised his hand to blow his horn
    And shout a "tally ho!"
    But mastered by that fox's eye
    His lips refused to blow;

11. For he was grim, and gaunt of limb
    With age all silvered o'er
    He might have been an Arctic fox
    Escaped from Greenland's shore.

12. But age his vigour had not tamed
    Nor tamed his glittering eye,
    That shone with an unearthly fire –
    A fire could never die.

13. And thus the huntsman he addressed
    In tones distinct and clear,
    Who heard as they who in a dream
    The fairies' music hear.

14. "Huntsman," he said – a sudden thrill
    Through all his listener ran
    To hear a creature of the wood
    Speak like a Christian man.

15. "Last of my race to me 'tis given,
    The future to unfold,
    To speak the words which never yet
    Spake fox of mortal mould.

16. "Then print my words upon your heart,
    And stamp them on your brain,
    That you to others may repeat
    My prophecy again.

17. "Strong life is yours, and manhood's prime
    Your cheek with health is red
    Time has not laid his finger yet,
    In earnest on your head.

18. "But ere your limbs are bent with age,
    And ere your locks are grey,
    The sport which you have loved so well,
    Shall long have passed away.

19. "Yet, think not, huntsman, I rejoice
    To see the end so near,
    Nor think the sound of horn or hound
    To me a sound of fear.

Rusty exploring in high summer.

A colourful hunting scene of 1901 that appeared in Vanity Fair
and showed "The Meet at Kirby Gate".

20. "How oft I've heard the Cotswold's cry,
    As Turner cheered the pack,
    And laughed to see his baffled hounds
    Hang vainly on my track.

21. "Then deem not that I speak in fear,
    Or prophesy in hate:
    Too well I know the doom reserved
    For all my tribe by fate.

22. "Too well I know, by wisdom taught,
    The existence of my race,
    O'er all wide England's green domain,
    Is bound up with the chase.

23. "Better in early youth and strength
    The race for life to run,
    Than poisoned like the noxious rat,
    Or slain by felon gun.

24. "Better by wily sleight and turn,
    The eager hound to foil,
    Than slaughtered by each baser churl
    Who yet shall till the soil.

25. "For not upon these hills alone,
    The doom of sport shall fall,
    O'er the broad face of England creeps
    The shadow on the wall.

26. "The years roll on; old manners change,
    Old customs lose their sway;
    New fashions rule; the grandsire's garb,
    Moves ridicule today.

27. "Time honoured creeds and ancient faith,
    The altar and the crown,
    Lordship, hereditary right,
    Before that tide go down.

28. "Base churls shall mock the mighty names
    Writ on the roll of time;
    Religion shall be held a jest,
    And loyalty a crime.

29. "No word of prayer, no hymn of praise,
    Sound in the village school;
    The people's education
    Utilitarians rule.

30. "In England's ancient pulpits
    Lay orators shall preach;
    New creeds and free religions
    Self made apostles teach.

31. "The peasants to their daily tasks
    In surly silence fall, –
    No kindly hospitalities
    In farmhouse or in hall.

32. "Nor harvest-feast, nor Christmas-tide,
    Shall farm or manor hold;
    Science alone can plenty give
    The only god is gold.

33. "The homes where love and peace should dwell
    Fierce politics shall vex,
    And unsexed woman strive to prove
    Herself the coarser sex.

34. "Mechanics in their workshops
    Affairs of state decide,
    Honour and truth old-fashioned words
    The noisy mobs deride.

35. "The statesmen that should rule the realm
    Coarse demagogues displace;
    The glory of a thousand years
    Shall end in foul disgrace.

36. "Trade shall be held the only good,
    And gain the sole device;
    The statesman's maxim shall be peace,
    And peace at any price.

37. "Her army and her navy,
    Britain shall cast aside;
    Soldiers and ships are costly things,
    Defence an empty pride.

38. "The German and the Muscovite
    Shall rule the narrow seas,
    Old England's flag shall cease to float
    In triumph on the breeze.

39. "The footsteps of the invader,
    Then England's shores shall know;
    While home-bred traitors give the hand
    To England's every foe.

40. "Disarmed before the foreigner
    The knee she'll humbly bend,
    And yield the treasures that she lacked
    The wisdom to defend.

41. "But not for aye, – yet once again,
    When purged by fire and sword
    The land her freedom shall regain,
    To manlier thoughts restored.

42. "Taught wisdom by disaster,
    England shall learn to know,
    That trade is not the only gain
    Heaven gives to man below.

43. "The greed for gold abated,
    The golden calf cast down,
    Old England's sons again shall raise
    The altar and the crown.

44. "Rejoicing seas shall welcome
    Their mistress once again;
    Again the banner of St. George
    Shall rule upon the main.

45. "The blood of the invader
    Her pastures shall manure;
    His bones unburied upon her fields,
    For monuments endure.

46. "Again in hall and homestead
    Shall joy and peace be seen,
    And smiling children raise again
    The maypole on the green.

47. "Again the hospitable board,
    Shall groan with Christmas cheer,
    And mutual service bind again
    The peasant and the peer.

48. "Again the smiling hedgerow
    Shall field from field divide.
    Again among the woodlands
    The scarlet troop shall ride.

49. "Again", – it seemed that aged fox
    More prophecies would say,
    When sudden came upon the wind,
    "Hark, forward! gone away!"

50. The listener started from his trance,
    He sat there all alone,
    That well-known cry had burst the spell,
    The aged fox was gone.

51. The huntsman turned, he spurred his steed,
    And to the cry he sped,
    And when he thought upon that fox,
    Said naught, but shook his head.

    D. W. Nash
    Cheltenham 1871

Reflections

This little book has been a genuine pleasure to write, as foxes have been, and still are, a real part of my life and have given me much enjoyment. I hope too that in a small way it will help to throw more light on the fox, its traditional place in the English landscape, and on those country people who love or hate the fox.

At the moment the gap between town and genuine country seems to be getting wider and so one of my aims has been to try and draw the two poles closer together. Unfortunately the drift apart is inevitable, but it can be overcome. The absence of understanding was shown to me some time ago, after I had written an article about foxes, mentioning "surplus killing". Because of this I received an irate letter from Birmingham telling me that this trait of fox behaviour was a myth put about by supporters of hunting. If only the writer had been right, we on our farm, including the hens, geese and guinea fowl would have been very happy.

More recently the Nature Correspondent of the *Daily Telegraph* received a letter which also illustrated a basic lack of knowledge. The letter writer had seen a fox in his garden and wanted to know if it was safe to put breast of mutton out for it as food – he was worried about the small bones. If he had stopped to think he would have realised that the natural diet of the fox contains many small, sharp bones, as well as some large ones, and it eats all with great enthusiasm. Where the concern originated from for giving dogs small bones is a mystery. Our dogs have all eaten a variety of bones from a very young age as part of their normal diet, as did my foxes, and we have never had a hint of trouble. So things that are obvious to country people pose problems to those living in towns; while difficult problems to the countryman often become quite incomprehensible to the townsman.

Because of society's urban and sub-urban orientation I also thought hard about whether I should include the chapter on hunting, for that is now surrounded by much prejudice both for and against. But as hunting and the fox have been linked for so long, its omission would have been wrong. Hunting no longer takes place near our farm, because of the proximity of a motorway, and in many ways we are sorry. Whether a fox was caught or not, the passing through of the hunt would always make the foxes more wary about coming into the farmyard with its barking dogs. Hunting it seems to me should be a question of personal choice. My own view is simple and straightforward; I do not hunt, but I agree with a biology lecturer who says:

> The fact that fox damage can be serious, even with control as at present, can be confirmed by reports from various organisations which run reserves – R.S.P.B., Nature Conservancy Council and local Naturalists' Trusts, etc.
>
> Of the various methods of fox control only hunting is biologically acceptable as it is as near to the natural process as possible, it cannot wound, doesn't kill or injure other species (as do traps, snares, poison, etc.) and tends to select out the old, sick, injured animals which are the very ones most likely to do damage.

Another gap I have tried to bridge is that of "ecological" fashion. More and more earnest people seem to be turning a love of the countryside into a clinical science, devoid of natural pleasure or spontaneous enjoyment. By so doing they erect a barrier that destroys the interest of many ordinary people, both young and old. As a result I have written a book about a common, beautiful wild animal, without feeling the need to use fashionable, pseudoscientific trans-Atlantic jargon words such as "vocalisation" and "interaction", neither have I felt the need to write the fox's

name in Latin, nor did I think that the reader needed to
know that botanists refer to the foxglove as *Digitalis pur-
purea*.

I am glad that as the book progressed I was not able to
throw light on some of the mysteries surrounding the fox.
Indeed, one became more of a puzzle, for as I wrote I
received several letters about fox/dog crosses. One said
quite categorically that foxes and dogs cannot mate, while
other writers as far apart as Scotland, Wales and Cornwall
disagreed. One correspondent sent me an engraving of a
fox/dog and another one, a photograph that appeared in the
Tatler of July 18th, 1923 of a cross between a tame dog fox
and a Cairn terrier bitch. A lady from London also informed
me of a man in Leicestershire who claimed to have crossed a
fox with a terrier: "The resultant offspring were very pretty
creatures," she wrote. "He gave one to his mother-in-law
and she was very fond of it. Unfortunately, as it got older, the
smell of fox grew even more pungent, but she refused to part
with it and as far as I know it lived to a ripe – in all senses –
old age."

Stories of the fox and the farmyard go back many years
into the past. I hope that they will go on far into the future.

Acknowledgments

I would like to thank, as usual, Teresa Brown for typing the final draft so well and so willingly, and those who read through the almost incomprehensible first draft – my mother, my sister Rachael and sister-in-law Ellen. In addition I would like to thank Dick Peel, Fiona Coulson, Jeremy Sorensen, Cyril Crow, "BB", Marcus and Daniel Webb, Brian Sewell, Mr. F. Newman, Betty Ogden, Bert Winchester, Mr. R. S. Lea, Mr. P. Heyworth, James Lowther, Mr. E. Merrick, Mr. John Robson M.F.H., Mr. C. S. Lawson, Mr. Kenneth N. Jennings, Mr. Bernard Sandle, Mr. Colin McIntyre, Mr. H. Thompson, Michelle Parrish, Mr. B. Tucks, Mrs. M. Holdeness, Dr. J. Fahey, Miss Audrey Clarke, Peter Thelwall, Albert Herridge, Arthur Illes and Mr. Duncan Birrell. I would also like to thank the *Daily Telegraph* for permission to use my articles on the Fernie Hunt and fox/dog crosses, and Christine Medcalf and Ion Trewin of Hodder & Stoughton for their help and enthusiasm.

I am indebted to several publishers and authors for permission to quote from the following books:

The Gingerbread Man (Ladybird Books).
Chicken Licken (Ladybird Books).
The Sly Fox and the Little Red Hen (Ladybird Books).
"The Three Little Foxes" from *When We Were Very Young*, by A. A. Milne (Methuen).
Fantastic Mr. Fox, by Roald Dahl (George Allen and Unwin).
The Canterbury Tales, by Geoffrey Chaucer, translated into modern English by Nevill Coghill (Penguin).

Selected Poems and Prose of John Clare, edited by Eric Robinson and Geoffrey Summerfield (Oxford University Press).
Wild Lone, by BB (Methuen).
The Ballad of the Belstone Fox, by David Rook (Hodder and Stoughton).
Reynard the Fox, by John Masefield (Heinemann).
Collected Rhymes and Verses, by Walter de la Mare (Faber).
The Society of Authors is also thanked for its permission to quote from the works of John Masefield and Walter de la Mare.

Short sections from my own books are included:
The death of Foss from *The Journal of a Country Parish* (Oxford University Press).
The First Hunt from *The Hunter and the Hunted*.
Cassius the first Cub from *The Decline of an English Village*.
Fox diet from *The Wildlife of the Royal Estates* (Hodder and Stoughton).

Illustrations Credits

Colour illustrations
Opposite p 32, G. Kinns/Biofotos; opposite p 33, Owen Newman/Nature Photographers Ltd; opposite p 48 (both), Michael Leach/Nature Photographers Ltd; opposite p 49, Owen Newman/Nature Photographers Ltd; opposite p 112 (both), Dr. Alan Beaumont; opposite p 113, Michael Leach/Nature Photographers Ltd; opposite p 128, Robin Page; opposite p 129, Mary Evans Picture Library.

Black and white illustrations
Special thanks to Brian Alderson for his invaluable help with the picture research.
Brian Alderson, pp 16, 21, 23, 29 (both), 31, 33, 34, 36, 37, 39, 44, 46; Michael Leach/Nature Photographers Ltd, pp 25, 58, 136; Natural History Museum, pp 27, 50; Heather Angel/Biofotos, p 54 (all); Holt Studios Ltd, p 59; Illustrated London News Picture Library, pp 64, 107, 114; Dr. Alan Beaumont, pp 68, 81; Mary Evans Picture Library, pp 73, 105; Robin Page, pp 84, 94, 95, 100; Emily Mayer, p 92.

Index

Figures in italics refer to captions